THE SALTWATER TACKLEBOX

THE
SALTWATER
TACKLEBOX

John Merwin

B. Mitchell

A FRIEDMAN GROUP BOOK

ISBN 0-88665-982-5

THE SALTWATER TACKLEBOX
was prepared and produced by
Michael Friedman Publishing Group, Inc.
15 West 26th Street
New York, New York 10010
for SMITHBOOKS LTD.
113 Merton Street
Toronto, Ontario
M4S 1A8

Editor: Elizabeth Viscott Sullivan
Art Director: Jeff Batzli
Designer: Bob Michaels
Photography Researcher: Daniella Jo Nilva

Typeset by The Typecrafters Inc.
Color separation by Scantrans Pte. Ltd.
Printed and bound in Hong Kong by Leefung-Asco Printers Ltd.

Contents

INTRODUCTION

Saltwater angling opportunities are incredibly diverse. Trolling for salmon off British Columbia has little in common with bait fishing for sheepshead off a Florida pier. Surf-casting for striped bass off the Nova Scotia coast is far removed from fly-casting for bonita off San Diego, California.

There is one common denominator, however, and that is fishing tackle. Understanding and using a spinning reel is no less important in Maine than it is in Florida, and the trolling tackle used for yellowfin tuna off Baja California is often the same as that used for sailfish off Mexico's Yucatán Peninsula. In addition, the considerations involved in selecting saltwater tackle and equipment are the same anywhere in the world. These considerations are what form the basis of this book. Every major category of saltwater tackle is described here in chapter-by-chapter coverage that applies to all fishing no matter where in the world that fishing might be.

Your particular saltwater fishing tackle must be appropriate for the type of fishing you will be doing. The fishing gear used for giant marlin off Australia, for example, is totally unsuited to catching flounder along the Massachusetts coast. Once the basic range of tackle is selected, the components must be balanced, which means the rod, reel, line, and accessory items must be in proportion and designed to work harmoniously with each other. Unbalanced tackle always works poorly and is a major hang-up for novice anglers, who often start fishing without the advice on tackle selection available in this book.

There are three major differences between freshwater and saltwater angling that anybody making the transition from fresh to salt needs to take into account. First, saltwater fishing is enormously varied, as the quarry may range from 2,000-pound (900-kg) marlin to snappers weighing only a few ounces. There is no equivalent to this wide range in fresh water, and thus the diversity of saltwater tackle is greater. This makes intelligent tackle choices even more difficult.

Pound for pound, virtually all saltwater fish are stronger than freshwater fish. The tackle

© Tony Mandile

you use for a 3-pound (1.4-kg) largemouth bass in fresh water might simply be destroyed when fighting a bonefish of similar size, for example. The plug-type lure you use to catch northern pike in fresh water can also be used to catch bluefish in salt water, as long as you realize that the substantially stronger bluefish might simply bite your lure in half. A more sturdy lure would be a better choice, of course.

Finally, salt water is substantially more corrosive than fresh water, and it takes a heavy toll on tackle. The metal parts of many freshwater reels and rods simply aren't designed to withstand saltwater corrosion, and some freshwater tackle may become rusted and useless almost overnight after exposure to the salt. The metals used in most saltwater tackle, such as anodized aluminum or stainless steel, are more resistant to corrosion, but even these will deteriorate unless some

care is taken. All tackle exposed to salt should be rinsed periodically and gently with fresh water. This simple act will add years of life to your tackle investment.

There are millions of saltwater anglers fishing along the world's coastlines. The majority of these anglers fish from shore or from bridges and piers. Many others pursue their sport with the aid of small boats on protected inshore waters such as bays and sounds. A relative few own or charter larger boats to seek offshore species such as tuna or marlin. Most of this book deals with light-tackle saltwater fishing in waters close to shore, because this is how most people fish. For the sake of completeness, I have described briefly the types of tackle used in offshore fisheries. Most people who go fishing offshore for the first time do so on a charter boat, where the tackle is provided and the captain's skills will compensate for their lack of experience.

*A hooked striped marlin takes
to the air.*

PART I
REELS

E ven though they may be relatively simple to use, most fishing reels are relatively complicated mechanical devices with gears, springs, clutches, levers, and cranks that are, for the most part, remarkably durable and trouble free. In saltwater use, corrosion caused by the salt is the major enemy of any reel. Most saltwater reels are made of corrosion-resistant materials such as stainless steel and aluminum, but even these are subject to corrosion if not maintained. The secret is a gentle rinsing at the end of every fishing day. The rinsing process should be a gentle one, however, because a powerful stream of rinse water, such as from a high-pressure hose, may have the unfortunate effect of forcing salt and sand deep into the reel mechanism.

Saltwater reels are made stronger than their freshwater counterparts simply because saltwater fish are generally larger and stronger than freshwater fish. Simple spin-casting reels that are used by millions of freshwater anglers are almost never seen in salt water. However, many larger spinning and conventional reels do see double duty in both coastal and inland waters. (Conventional reels are reels in which the reel spool revolves, as opposed to spinning reels, in which the spool is fixed. Conventional reels include bait-casting, trolling, and bottom-fishing reels; "conventional reel" is the general term, and will be used throughout this book.) Generally if any reel can accommodate at least 200 yards (183 m) of 12-pound-test (5.4-kg-test), it's a safe bet for light-tackle saltwater use as long as the usual maintenance precautions are followed.

*Freshwater anglers just don't understand
what saltwater fish can do to their tackle...*
— Bernard "Lefty" Kreh

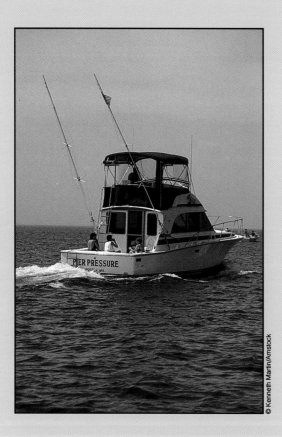

Chapter 1
Spinning Reels

Of the two basic types of saltwater reels, spinning reels are by far the newest. Spinning didn't become widely popular until the introduction of monofilament nylon lines after World War II, even though the basic reel design had been developed many years earlier. Spinning is now the most common saltwater-fishing method.

Understanding how these reels work is essential to your success. The term spinning as it applies to a fishing reel probably takes its name from the late nineteenth-century textile industry, as various techniques which the textile industry developed for handling large spools of thread form the basis of the reel design. When casting and retrieving line, the spinning reel's spool remains fixed, unlike conventional reels in which the spool itself is turned to recover line. In a spinning reel, a line roller is attached to a gear-driven cup and revolves around the stationary spinning reel spool. This action winds line on the spool when the reel handle is turned. At the same time, another gear oscillates the spool up and down within the cup so that the line is wound evenly up and down the spool's depth. This ensures that each succeeding layer of line isn't crammed into the underlying layers and allows line to flow freely over the end of the spool when a lure or bait is cast. Because the line can flow or spin freely over the end of the fixed spool in the act of casting a weight, there is relatively little friction, and light lures can be cast for a considerable distance. Ultralight spinning reels, for example, can be used to cast lures weighing as little as $\frac{1}{32}$

ounce (.88 g), assuming a correspondingly light (such as 2-pound-test [1-kg-test]) line is used. Casting such light lures is almost impossible with anything else except for fly tackle.

Although light lures and light lines were part of their original appeal, spinning reels quickly underwent a variety of design modifications to accommodate different kinds of fishing tactics. There's now a wide range of spinning-reel models suitable for everything from tiny snappers to small marlin.

All spinning reels have a number of features in common that you should be familiar with. First, they have a reel "foot" that consists of a short, solid shaft perpendicular to the reel body that leads to a flat narrow plate. The flat narrow portion is what goes into the reelseat on the rod. The reel handle is usually on the left side of the reel body for right-handed casters, who would normally be turning the reel handle with their left hands. Left-handers can switch the handle on most reels. Many spinning reels have the spool surrounded, not by a traditional cup, but by a rotating armature that turns around both the spool and a bowl-like extension on the bottom of the spool, called a "skirt." Such skirted-spool reels are less prone to tangling since loose line can't get underneath the spool. For a given size reel, skirted spools are usually smaller in diameter than regular spools, and therefore tend to shorten casting distance. For most fishing, this doesn't make much dif-

ference and the tangle-free features of skirted-spool reels have made them very popular.

There are times, such as when surf-casting, when this slight difference can be critical. Lou Baballe and I were surf fishing one foggy September morning on Cape Cod's outer beaches, where we could see bluefish feeding near an offshore bar. After he had taken three fish to my none, I walked down the beach to find out what I was doing wrong.

A skirted-spool spinning reel such as this one (below) is commonly used in surf-casting (opposite page).

These are premium saltwater spinning reels in a range of sizes.

He stopped fishing as I approached and watched me cast. "You're too short," he said, pointing at my new, skirted-spool reel. "Our reels are about the same size, but the regular spool on my older reel is larger in diameter so I can cast farther. Here's a lure just like mine. Put it on and let's try it together."

We both cast hard and watched the lures splash down near the bar. He was obviously reaching about 30 feet (9 m) beyond my longest cast and promptly hooked what proved to be the last bluefish of the morning. That afternoon, of course, I changed reels and have used regular spinning reels when surf-casting ever since.

With both skirted-spool and regular spinning reels, there's a bail and line roller assembly that looks like a bucket handle (hence the name "bail") around the side of the spool. If you lift this upward, you'll feel a click as it fastens and holds in a vertical, open position. After a cast is made, a slight turn of the reel handle clicks the bail shut. When it shuts, the bail captures the line and slides it under the line roller. Make sure your line roller is perfectly smooth—not chipped or scratched—and turns freely if it's designed to do so. Inadequate or damaged line rollers are the prime cause of line failure on spinning reels.

Almost all spinning reels are available with easily interchangeable line spools, which means you can keep spare spools loaded with lighter or heavier line for use with different sized lures. It's also an advantage to be able to change to a fresh spool quickly if the one you're using becomes irrevocably snarled when the fishing action is fast and furious. So when selecting a spinning reel, try to obtain one or two extra spools at the same time.

Spinning reels don't usually come filled with line. Many tackle shops and a few mail-order houses, however, will use a mechanical line-winding device to fill your reel for a nominal fee. This is the most economical approach, since you'll get exactly the right amount of line correctly installed with no waste and no twists. Spare spools can be filled in the same manner with the line you specify.

Sooner or later, however, you're going to have to spool your own spinning reels. There are a few precautions you must observe to avoid line twist and to ensure optimum performance. First, mount the reel on the rod. Spinning reels are designed to mount under the rod grip so that both the reel and the line guides are on the same side. If the reelseat is in a fixed position, you can't adjust it. If the reelseat is two sliding rings over a cork or synthetic handle, mount the reel in the middle of the handle, securing each end of the reel foot with one of the sliding rings. You may later wish to move the reel slightly forward of center for better balance in casting. Next, thread the line through the first guide and then use an Arbor Knot (page 123) to secure the line to the reel spool. Be sure to

Courtesy Penn Fishing Tackle Mfg. Co.

open the bail before you attach the line to the spool so you'll then be able to wind on the line after the bail is closed.

The easiest method at this point is to lay the line spool flat on the floor and start cranking in line with the reel. Be sure to have the line running through your fingers under a slight tension as it goes on the reel so the line spools evenly. After a few turns, stop cranking and allow a little slack to fall between the reel and line spool. If the slack line twists, you're taking line off the spool in the wrong direction; turn the line spool over to make line come off of it in the opposite direction before you continue cranking.

Continue filling the reel spool—remembering to keep slight tension on the incoming line—until it's filled to within $\frac{1}{8}$ inch (3 mm) of the rim. Spools filled more than this tend to release loops of slack line when casting. Spools filled less than this will reduce your effective casting distance through friction against the spool rim. Be very careful in this process to avoid both slack winds on the reel

This is a regular spinning reel in which the spool is enclosed by a revolving cup.

© Hanson Carroll

spool and twisting the line. If either happens, your reel will be plagued by frequent and annoying line tangles.

When your reel spool is full, cut the line and secure the loose end on the spool with a rubber band. Now you can fill your spare spools with the same or a different size line, depending on your needs. After each spool is full, mark a small piece of tape with the line weight and date installed and fasten it to the underside of the spool in such a way that the tape won't interfere with the spool's operation. You'll need this information later when it's time to check or change your line, and—if you have more than one spool for the same reel—it will enable you to keep track of

A skirted-spool spinning reel (below) is generally more tangle-free than a regular-type reel (opposite page).

Courtesy Shimano American

what's on your spare spools.

All spinning reels have an anti-reverse feature. This keeps the handle from turning backward and whacking your knuckles when you hook a strong fish, and it makes sure the fish is pulling against the reel's drag instead of causing the entire reel mechanism to spin backward. This same feature also helps to keep the bail from closing unexpectedly when you're casting. If this happens with heavier lures, the line may snap and you'll lose your lure. The anti-reverse on most reels is turned on and off with a sliding switch or lever at the rear of the reel body. You should leave your anti-reverse on at all times unless you have a specific reason for not doing so, such as turn-

Trolling off the Hawaiian coast.

ing the handle backward while working on a line tangle.

Drag adjustment on most spinning reels is conducted by means of a knob on top of the reel spool. Some reels have this adjustment at the rearmost portion of the reel body. In either case, turning the knob clockwise tight-ens the drag while a counterclockwise turn loosens the drag. As with most other reel types, set your drag to 25 to 30 percent of your line's rated break strength. This will allow a strong fish to pull line from the reel in a controlled fashion while you stay connected. Never try to increase the drag adjustment while you're playing a fish. Instead, apply additional drag tension by using the fingers of your left hand as a brake against the reel spool. If the fish makes a sudden lunge, you can back off the extra tension instantly and avoid a broken line.

Casting with a spinning reel is very simple. String the line through the guides and use a Trilene Knot (page 123) to attach a black snap swivel (page 121) to the end of the line. Then attach a practice casting weight of a size appropriate to your outfit. A ⅜-ounce (9.5-g) weight is good for most medium-weight (single-handed) saltwater rods and reels. Hold the rod and reel in your right hand with the reel stem between your second and third fingers. Reel the practice weight up to within 4 to 6 inches (10 to 15 cm) of the rod tip. Use your right index finger to hold the line while your left hand cocks the bail open. Make sure the line is resting on the fleshy part of your fingertip and isn't caught down in the finger's first joint. Some spinning reels have a trigger device on the bail that allows you to capture the line with your right index finger and open the bail simultaneously with the same finger.

Now bring the rod gently back overhead to a 45-degree angle behind you. Look around to make sure you won't hit anything when you bring the rod forward. Now, aim at a target 30 to 40 feet (9 to 12 m) distant and bring the rod sharply and smoothly forward. Stop abruptly and simultaneously release the line when the rod is about 45 degrees in front of you. The practice weight will fly through the air as soon as you release the line held by

Medium-weight spinning tackle is ideal for a wide variety of inshore species.

your right index finger.

It's easy, once again, to tell what's going wrong if you're having problems. If the weight goes out in a high looping trajectory on the

Heading out of a New Jersey fishing port, where bluefish are a primary target.

cast, you're letting go with your index finger too soon. If the weight darts into the ground in front of you, you're releasing too late. As with most lure casts, the practice weight should go to the target in a low, flat trajectory. Spinning reels do offer the advantage of being able to control the flight of the lure to a certain extent. If it appears that you're going to overshoot the target, just extend your right index finger to the lip of the spool to slow the line as it comes off, thereby shortening the cast in midair. Many experts with spinning gear can hit a coffee cup consistently at 60 feet (18 m). Such accuracy can be very important in many kinds of fishing. Your own practice can pay big dividends.

Surf-casting with large two-handed rods (page 62) is essentially the same process. In this case, however, your left hand will be on the lower portion of the rod grip as you bring the rod back to cast. On the forward power stroke, pull the butt of the rod sharply toward you with your left hand while your right hand is pushing above to bring the rod forward smartly, followed by an abrupt stop and release of the lure. Throwing the heavier lures used in surf-casting can put consider-

Sunrise along the Hawaiian coast.

able stress on the tip of your casting finger. I often wrap the tip of my right index finger with waterproof bandage tape to keep from getting a blister.

When you're moving slowly and looking for fish, whether walking a northern beach or cruising a shallow, tropical flat, you should keep your bail open and be ready to cast instantly. Many saltwater fish move rapidly when feeding, and you'll need to cast quickly and accurately when you see them. Taking the time to open your bail and get ready to cast can often mean a missed fish.

One common mistake that's made with spinning reels is turning the reel handle while a large fish is pulling line against the drag system. This will usually twist the line so badly that you'll wind up having to throw the line away. It's important to remember to retrieve line only when the fish is coming toward you. With the large, powerful fish commonly found in salt water, you can use a technique called "pumping." Lift the rod against the strain of the fish without reeling. Then lower the rod quickly, reducing the line strain, and reel rapidly at the same time. Repeating this process a number of times will usually allow you to work a heavy fish toward shore or your boat in the latter stages of a long fight.

Once you learn how to handle a revolving spool (casting reel), you have greater control under more different circumstances than you do with a spinning reel.

— Frank Woolner

Chapter 2
Conventional Reels

Conventional reels are those in which the spool revolves in casting and retrieving line, as opposed to spinning reels in which the spool is fixed. While spinning reels are used for relatively light-tackle casting in salt water, including surf-casting, conventional reels are traditionally used for bottom fishing and trolling. Between 1950 and 1970, spinning reels eclipsed conventional models for casting in salt water, but because conventional reels are so well adapted to fighting big, strong fish, they are now being used again for saltwater casting.

Conventional saltwater reels between the Civil War and the 1920s were gleaming models of black hard rubber and nickel silver or aluminum. Perhaps the best models were those made by the Vom Hofe family, first in New York and later in Philadelphia. Initially, these reels had no drag systems other than a simple click. Instead, they featured a "thumb-stall," a leather pad that could be pressed with one's thumb against the spool to slow the run of a fish. Aside from the numerous burns and cuts on one's hands this method caused, it also meant that really strong fish, such as the southern tarpon that was becoming popular by the 1880s, were rarely landed. They were simply too strong for that type of tackle. The most important development in saltwater reels was the star drag, often attributed to the Vom Hofes around the turn of the century. This drag system featured a wide adjustment range, which meant that even marlin weighing half a ton (453 kg) could be successfully fought. Star drags, which use

*These conventional-style reels
are used strictly for big-game
trolling.*

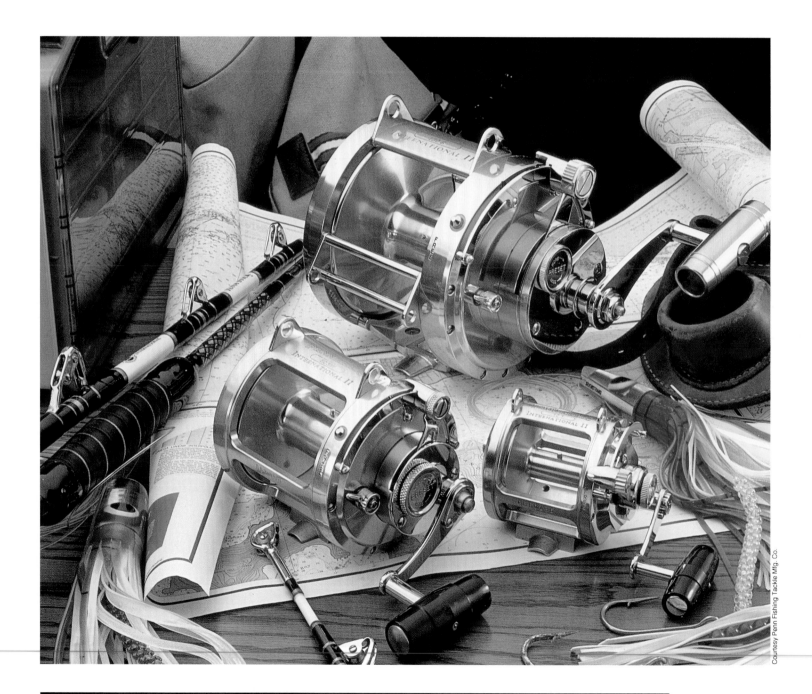

adjustable friction discs to put a precisely set tension on outgoing line, are a nearly universal feature now on all conventional saltwater reels.

Modern reels fall into three basic categories. There are those for light-tackle casting (including surf-casting), which include many freshwater bait-casting reels. There are also reels mostly suited to bottom fishing, and some made especially for light- or heavy-duty offshore trolling. Many of these reels have mechanical features in common, so here's a review of them, using contemporary bait-casting reels as an example.

Modern bait-casting reels are engineering marvels, but perhaps no more so than the first such reel, which was made by George Snyder, a Kentucky watchmaker, in 1810. This reel differed from earlier brass British reels in two important respects. Snyder's reel was sufficiently smooth-running that a bait could be cast from the reel itself. Earlier reels were so rough that line had to be pulled from the reel, held, and then released by hand in order to cast. Snyder's reel was also a multiplier; that is, the line spool revolved more than once for every turn of the reel handle, as opposed to earlier reels that were all single-actioned (one spool revolution for every turn of the handle). Bait-casting reels soon came to be 4:1 multipliers, with 4 spool revolutions per handle turn; some modern models offer higher ratios. Soon there were other watchmakers in the reel trade, notably C. F. Millam

This conventional reel is suitable for either casting or trolling.

Courtesy Shimano American

and J. F. and B. F. Meek, and by the end of the Civil War these reels had become an American standard.

These early reels were first used for fishing with bait, hence the name bait-casting. When bass plugs came into vogue after 1900, the same reels were often called plug-casting reels. Today, they're used for many types of saltwater fishing.

Casting reels require more skill than spinning reels. Many anglers find the mastery of this skill to be especially rewarding. These

TUNA

There are several kinds of tuna of importance to anglers, ranging from giant bluefins that may top out at 1,400 pounds (634 kg) down to small bonita of 3 to 6 pounds (1.4 to 2.7 kg) that challenge fly anglers in both New England and southern California. In the United States, albacore (the "white-meat" tuna) are a mainstay of west-coast anglers in the summer and early fall, while yellowfin tuna are sought on both coasts, usually well offshore.

In general, most tuna fishing is done with trolled baits or lures at relatively high speed, although once a school of fish is located, more effective live baits may be cast or trolled around the edges of the school. Still fishing with live baits at various depths is commonly done for bluefin tuna in the northeast section of North America as an alternative to trolling, which can also be effective. All tuna are exceptionally streamlined and powerful, designed for extended high-speed swimming in the open ocean. The body fins of many tuna, for example, fold into slots along the body during rapid swimming. A tuna's tail has evolved into a highly efficient crescent shape and is linked to the tuna's powerful muscles through a thin wrist of strong tendons, which work like a pulley to provide a mechanical advantage in swimming.

Courtesy Penn Fishing Tackle Mfg. Co.

These conventional reels offer the utmost in casting distance with heavy lures or natural baits.

Courtesy Penn Fishing Tackle Mfg. Co.

These premium reels don't have level-wind devices, so the line must be spooled evenly by hand.

control of the spool when casting. Most reels have mechanical anti-backlash devices built in that help in this regard, but no such device completely eliminates the need for a practiced and "educated" thumb in casting.

Light-tackle casting reels, such as those commonly used for striped bass or small tarpon, are mounted on top of a rod with a distinctive trigger-type reelseat. These reels have a flat, elongated foot that fits into the reelseat, usually held by a screw-locking device or a clamp. A right-handed reel has its handles on the right side when correctly mounted. Almost all casting reels feature a level-wind device that moves back and forth in front of the spool when the reel handle is turned, making sure that the line is evenly spooled on the reel. You may eventually encounter a casting reel without such a device, but be forewarned; these are for experts only. Changing spools on casting reels involves unscrewing and removing one sideplate and is a general pain in the neck on most models. I've found it simpler over the years to have a complete spare reel, if need be, instead of trying to change spools.

Casting reels don't come filled with line and, again, the easiest thing is to have the reel filled with the desired line type at the store where you buy the reel. As usual, though, you're going to have to do this yourself sooner or later, so here's how. Mount the reel on the rod. Thread the line through the rod guides, then through the level-wind de-

reels offer the advantage of the greatest casting accuracy, allow the use of heavier line for a given lure weight, and are the most efficient fighting tools when dealing with large fish. Because the spool revolves when the lure or bait is pulling out line during the cast, the spool itself can overrun and, if not controlled, will produce a line tangle called a backlash. Backlashes are avoided by precise thumb

vice, and fasten it to the reel spool with an Arbor Knot (page 123). Have an assistant poke a pencil or similar object through the small hole in the center of the line spool so the spool can revolve on this axis when you're cranking the reel handle. Your helper should apply a slight, yet constant tension to the line spool while you're winding, so the line goes on the reel evenly. Keep cranking until the spool is filled to within ⅛ to 1/16 of an inch (⅓ to ⅛ of a cm) of the spool's edge, then clip the line and secure the loose end with a rubber band for the time being. When you're filling the spool, make sure the line spool and reel spool are both turning in the same direction to avoid line twist. If they're not, turn the line spool around and then continue.

As with all types of reels, filling with too little line will reduce your casting efficiency. Using too much line will produce tangles. Overfilling casting reels can allow slack line to slip between the reel spool and the frame, and you'll have to take the reel apart to solve this problem if and when it occurs. Premium reels minimize this problem with fine tolerances and very little space between the reel spool and frame.

Most casting reels now have a free-spool button or similar device at the right rear of the reel frame. This disengages the handle and drive gears when a cast is made and allows the spool to turn more freely, thus producing smoother and longer casts. There should also be—and usually is—a built-in anti-reverse that keeps the handle from turning backward when you're reeling in or fighting a fish. The fish, of course, should only be pulling line out against the reel's drag. Without an anti-reverse, the reel handle could spin suddenly backward and deliver a painful rap to your knuckles, as well as tangle the line, and cause you to lose the fish. If your anti-reverse can be turned on and off, leave it on at all times.

The price of not using your anti-reverse can be high. Once my friend Rudy Rughoff and I were fishing in an estuary off the Gulf of Mexico. Traveling in separate skiffs with our respective guides, we found some tarpon rolling and feeding on what appeared to be sardines. The sun was setting at our backs and made the fishes' silver scales glow with gold as the fish rolled up through the water's surface.

Rudy was getting so excited that he botched the first cast. On his second try, a tarpon took his lure in a swift roll and then jumped high as Rudy set the hook hard. The fish ran fast, swiftly spinning his reel handles backward as line paid out freely—and with no drag—because he had forgotten to check his anti-reverse switch. Rudy reached for the reel and screamed, as the rapidly spinning handles caught his thumb. He doubled over and clutched his hand as the rod dropped to the boat's bottom and the line broke. By the time we had run the boats back to our fishing-resort camp, Rudy's thumb was tremendously

Note the star-shaped drag adjustment wheel on the reel at far left — this is typical of conventional models.

swollen, and he had to be driven 80 miles (128 km) north to the nearest hospital to have his broken thumb set and splinted.

Rudy still uses a conventional casting reel on big fish. But he learned his lesson the hard way. Instead of grabbing the reel handle when fighting a strong running fish, he should have let the reel's anti-reverse and drag settings do the work.

Almost all casting reels have a star drag that's adjusted with a star-shaped wheel between the reel handle and sideplate. Set your drag to 25 to 30 percent of your line's rated breaking strength. As usual, don't try to change the drag adjustment when you're fighting a fish. It's very simple to apply additional pressure on the reel spool with your thumb to put more pressure on a fish. This sort of supplemental drag and precise control is most easily done with casting reels and is a big advantage when fishing for outsize tarpon, bluefish, or striped bass. If I were fishing for a trophy fish of any kind and wanted to be most certain of landing it, I'd use a conventional reel.

Using a casting reel is more complicated than spinning, but many people find the added control to be worth the effort and time spent practicing. Start by threading the line through the rod guides and use a Trilene Knot (page 123) to attach a black snap swivel (page 121) to the end of the line. For most medium-weight saltwater outfits, beginners will find a ⅝-ounce (17-g) practice weight

easiest, assuming the rod is calibered for this weight. Go heavier or lighter depending on your outfit.

Reel the weight up to within 6 inches (15 cm) of the rod tip. Now adjust your cast-control knob (anti-backlash device) so that when the reel is in free spool the weight will descend slowly to the ground. If the casting weight won't descend of its own accord, your setting is too tight. If it moves rapidly downward, tighten your cast control a little and try again. If you're practicing on a windy day, set yourself up to cast with the wind at your back.

Grip the rod in your right hand with the reel handles on top, your right index finger on the reelseat trigger, and your right thumb resting on the lowermost edge of the reel spool. Press your thumb against the spool to keep it from moving while you press the free-spool button with your left hand. Raise your forearm and bend your wrist slightly to bring the rod vertically behind you to about a 45-degree angle. Look around to make sure you won't hit anything when you cast except your target about 40 feet (12 m) away.

Bring the rod sharply forward with a chopping motion of your arm and wrist and stop abruptly when the rod is 45 degrees in front. As you stop, release almost all of your thumb pressure from the spool. If you remove your thumb completely from the spool it will overrun and backlash. If you press too hard against the spool, it won't turn and the casting weight won't go anywhere. The lightest

Courtesy Penn Fishing Tackle Mfg. Co.

These heavy-duty reels find use in trolling for everything from bluefish to sailfish.

Gradually increase your thumb pressure during the cast so that the spool is stopped at the same instant that the weight stops. The beauty of this method is that you're in complete control of the cast at all times. You can stop the casting weight (or lure or bait) at any point in its flight with simple thumb pressure and thus be exceptionally accurate.

Backlashes can rival a bird's nest for complexity; and you'll have plenty of practice in untangling them. Some beginners are helped by tightening the cast control on their reels more than normal when starting out and loosening that control to a lighter, more appropriate setting as proficiency is gained. The greatest difficulty comes in using lures or baits that are too light; these require the most finely attuned thumb. Casting into a stiff breeze is also troublesome, since the wind will slow the lure's flight prematurely and your reel-thumbing will have to compensate for this. If I have to fish in a strong headwind, I usually switch to spinning tackle.

After your cast, switch the reel and rod to your left hand. Cup the left side of the reel against your palm and use your left thumb and index finger to apply a little tension to the line as you retrieve the casting weight. The rod is supported by the remaining three fingers of your left hand under the reel and rod while you turn the reel handle with your right hand. This is called a "palming grip" because of the position of your left hand. Alternatively, and with casting rods that have a fairly long

pressure of your thumb will help you keep control of the turning spool. This touch comes with practice. I have watched superb anglers and champion tournament casters get their share of backlashes. It happens to everyone, so don't be discouraged.

As the casting weight flies to the target, its speed diminishes. If left alone, the speed of the rotating reel spool will diminish more slowly and thus overrun. If you don't thumb the spool during the cast, you'll backlash.

*Successful offshore trolling
usually means starting early.*

(or two-handed) rear grip, you can use your left hand on the small grip in front of the reel while using your thumb and forefinger to apply tension as just described. In this case, the butt of the rod should be braced against your lower abdomen.

Casting reels are most effective when used with relatively heavy line weights and lures. The lighter the line and lure, the greater the difficulty in casting with these reels. Happily, the reels readily adapt to heavier lines (10- to 25-pound-test [4.5- to 11-kg-test] and heavier) by virtue of their revolving spools. While heavy lines diminish the effectiveness of fixed-spool spinning reels through friction, the friction factor of a revolving spool is the same regardless of line size (within reasonable limits), and the angler's options are correspondingly greater. With heavier baits and lures (to about 6 ounces [169 g]) it's possible to cast farther in the surf with conventional reels than with spinning reels, as long as you're not bucking a headwind.

Casting reels for salt water can range from medium-size freshwater models accommodating 200 yards (183 m) of 10- to 12-pound-test (4.5- to 5.4-kg-test) line up to larger versions for surf-casting that may take 300 yards (274 m) of 30-pound-test (14-kg-test) monofilament or even more. Larger reels often don't have level-wind devices and you'll have to remember to spool the line evenly

with your hand in front of the reel when retrieving line.

Reels for pier and bottom fishing can be less sophisticated, as long-distance casting isn't usually a criterion. However, since I use most of my reels in a variety of ways, I wind up using my casting reels when I go bottom fishing for flounder, for example, rather than buying an additional, less expensive reel for the same purpose.

Trolling reels, including those that are used in the now-popular stand-up fishing for tuna, California yellowtails, and many other pelagic fishes, are characterized by their sophisticated drag systems, quality gearing, and heavy-duty construction. They are not used for casting, for their primary functions are strength and smoothness in fighting the big fish that put extraordinary stress on any reel. These reels are generally designated according to the size of line usually used on each. The smallest is typically a 20-pound (9-kg) reel, which doesn't weigh 20 pounds of course, but is designed to be used with 20-pound-test line. Additional models often include, 30-, 50-, 80-, and 130-pound (14-, 22-, 36-, and 59-kg) reels, which correspond to the record-fish/line weight categories maintained by the International Game Fish Association in Florida. Reel size and line capacity increase dramatically with the line-size designation.

The rock (striper) takes a bait readily; and, from the vigor of its actions, affords fine sport with the rod and reel; the fly especially adapted to the capture of this species...

— **Spencer Fullerton Baird (1855)**

Chapter 3
Saltwater Fly Reels

With the various kinds of saltwater reels reviewed in previous chapters, a weighted lure is used in casting to pull line from the reel, or line is simply released for trolling. Fly casting is quite different. In this case, a nearly weightless fly or bug is carried through the air by a heavy line; in other words, the line itself is the casting weight and the fly goes along for the ride. Among other things, this means that fly reels aren't used for casting at all and, for most saltwater applications, are the simplest of all reels.

The fly reel has three essential functions in fly fishing. It provides adequate storage space for a bulky fly line that is pulled from the reel by hand before the cast is made. It allows larger fish to be played from the reel and may even incorporate a drag system for this purpose. It serves to counterbalance the weight of the fly rod that extends for many feet beyond the angler's hand and reel.

Fly reels are generally narrow in proportion to their diameter and many are "ventilated" with numerous holes drilled in the sideplates. Ventilated sideplates were originally developed to aid in the air-drying of the older silk fly lines that rotted if they were not dried after use. With modern synthetic lines, these holes serve no other purpose than to lighten the reel. Many saltwater fly reels are now made without these holes.

The reel spool revolves on a central spindle, which should be kept clean and lightly lubricated for optimum performance. Most fly-reel models easily accommodate spare

This ultra-premium fly reel features a smooth drag and line capacity sufficient for big tarpon and sailfish.

spools; since many fly-casters use more than one type of line (floating and sinking versions, for example), a spare spool is desirable.

Most fly reels are of a single-action design, which means that the reel spool revolves once for every turn of the handle. A few fly-reel models have multiplying gears, or multipliers, that allow line to be reeled in more quickly. This is especially helpful in recovering line after a bonefish has run off 200 yards

(183 m) of line. In general, however, multipliers aren't as strong as single-action designs, which make the latter preferable for tough fish such as tarpon and large striped bass. Some reels have an anti-reverse feature,

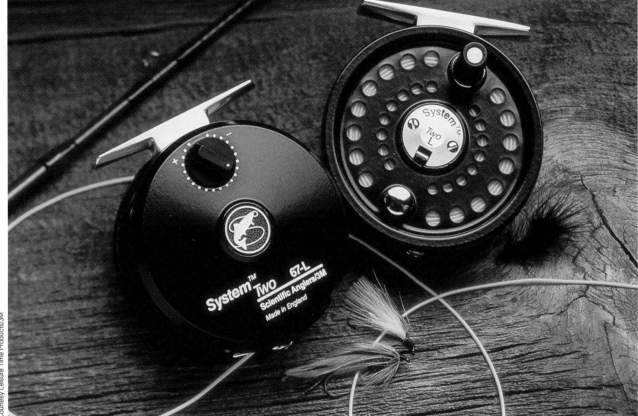

Courtesy Leisure Time Products/3M

which keeps the reel handle stationary while a fish pulls line out against the drag mechanism. Other models, called direct-drive models, allow the reel handle to turn when line is pulled out. Anti-reverse features are a convenience, but direct drive is stronger and is best for the largest fish.

Fly reels are designed to be mounted under and at the rear of the rod with the reelseat behind the rod grip. The winding handle

This reel's drag mechanism is adjusted by turning the small knob near the reel foot.

may be on the right or left side as you prefer. Try using the reel with its handle on the left side first (for right-handed anglers) so you don't have to switch the rod from your right to your left hand to wind up line or play a fish. On most rods the reel foot locks into the reelseat by means of threaded rings. Some light freshwater models have a pair of sliding bands for the same purpose, but these aren't strong enough for saltwater use. There are a few fly reels whose feet don't fit all reelseats. This is less common than in past years, but it still pays to make sure that your new reel will fit on your new rod before you buy either.

Most times, you'll have to use some backing line when filling your fly reel, as most fly lines are only about 90 feet (27 m) long. Backing is a fine-diameter line spooled on the reel under the fly line. Backing line allows you to handle large, long-running fish and also ensures that the reel itself is filled to capacity. If the reel is only partly full, the effective circumference of the spool is reduced, causing you to retrieve line at a slower rate. A partly full spool also means the fly line will be stored in smaller coils. These small coils will be retained in the line after being pulled from the spool for casting.

Most reel makers specify how much backing a particular reel will accommodate in addition to what size fly line should be used. This makes it relatively easy to fill a reel. If you don't know how much backing your reel will take, the most accurate way of filling the reel is to first wind on the fly line, and then wind backing on top of the fly line until the reel is full. Then you'll have to reverse the lines so the backing is underneath the fly line.

Courtesy Scientific Anglers

The drag on this particular model is caliper-based, just like a car's disc brakes.

It's easiest to fill your reel when it's on the rod. First mount the reel; thread the backing line through the first butt guide, and attach it to the reel spool with an Arbor Knot (page 123). Use 30-pound-test (14-kg-test) braided Dacron backing line sold specifically for this purpose. Some reel makers recommend 20-pound-test (9-kg-test) backing, but 30-pound backing will tangle less often because of its larger diameter. Ask a friend to poke a

*This heavy fly outfit is set up
and ready for offshore
billfishing.*

When the correct amount of backing is spooled (again, see the instructions that came with your reel), clip the line and attach the fly line to the backing with an Albright Knot (page 123). Most new fly lines have a small tag on one end that indicates which end should be attached to the backing. (With some lines, if you attach the wrong end, the fly-line taper will be reversed and you won't be able to cast it very well.) Now wind on the fly line as you did the backing (with a pencil through the line spool), again being careful to avoid line twist. The entire fly line should fit on the reel to within ⅛ inch (3 mm) or so of the spool edge. The spool should turn freely without any line binding against the reel frame. If the entire line doesn't fit, don't cut it. Its continuous taper is important for casting. Instead, remove the fly line and then remove enough backing so you can install the complete fly line.

Using the wrong backing line can be expensive, as my neighbor Don Wetzel found out on a recent bonefishing trip. It was his first bonefishing trip, and to save money he used some heavy nylon monofilament line instead of Dacron™ for backing on a new, $200 fly reel. He finally hooked a bonefish that ran off 150 yards (137 m) of backing line, which Don then reeled back in under tension as he played the fish. Monofilament stretches under tension, which means he put all that line on his reel when it was stretched. When he

pencil or similar object through the backing-line spool and apply a little tension to the line while you wind it on the reel. If you're winding with your left hand, use the fingers of your right hand to move the line back and forth as you wind so the line spools on the reel evenly. Make sure the backing spool and reel spool are turning in the same direction to avoid line twist.

went to use the reel a second time, the spool was bent and cracked in half, totally destroyed by the contraction of stretched monofilament. He learned, as many do, that braided Dacron™ must be used as backing line because Dacron™ doesn't stretch and contract to any great degree.

The next step is to attach a leader to the fly line. A leader is a tapered length of monofilament from 7½ to 12 feet (2.2 to 3.6 m) long that provides a nearly invisible link between fly line and fly. The leader's taper helps the fly to "turn over," that is, lie straight out from the line at the end of a cast. The butt end, the thickest portion of the leader should be attached to the end of the fly line with a Nail Knot (page 123).

The most basic saltwater fly reels have a simple, click-type drag system based on a triangular metal pawl that is held against a gear on the back of the spool by a light spring. This type of drag makes the reel click in both directions and offers slightly more resistance to outgoing line than when the line is reeled in. On many reels this click tension is adjustable. Set yours only tight enough to prevent the reel from overrunning when you give a sudden jerk on the line. Your fingers can pro-

vide additional tension when you're playing a fish. You can either clamp the line down on the rod grip or use your fingers to put pressure against the inside of the spool. In either case, you'll find the sensitivity of your hand and fingers offers a responsive drag.

Some reels have more sophisticated drag systems that are based on the compression of internal drag washers or caliper-based systems that work much like the disc brakes on a car. With these types of systems, the drag adjustment should be light; that is, it should be only tight enough to keep the spool from overrunning. Again, the best way of applying additional drag is with your fingertips on the line or spool. Many fly anglers make the mistake of using much too tight a drag setting. This makes little difference for small fish, but when a really big one is hooked, the high drag setting will almost certainly cause the hook to pull free or a knot to fail.

A saltwater reel should accommodate 200 yards (183 m) of backing plus the fly line. You won't need all that backing when you're catching small bonefish, striped bass, or bluefish, but larger versions of the same or other species may force you to use every inch of that backing.

**Dolphin are a popular offshore
fly-rod fish.**

PART II
RODS

Trying to choose a rod from the hundreds on display in a modern saltwater tackle shop can be a tough chore for anyone. Fortunately, most merchants organize their rod displays by rod type, which means that the following chapters can help you narrow the choices very quickly. There are also a few simple rules in these pages for rod selection that can help you to further narrow things down to a handful of different models among which the only consideration may be price.

In general, you get what you pay for in terms of rod quality. Rods are generally less subject to saltwater corrosion problems than reels since the only metal parts on rods are the reelseat and the line guides. The usual maintenance precaution of a periodic fresh-water rinse will keep most rods in relatively good condition. The quality of the rod you require, and the price, will increase according to the size and toughness of the fish you're going after. An inexpensive rod may give years of service in bottom fishing for small flounder, for example; however, the same rod may shatter with the first explosive run of a bluefish or a tarpon. It would seem silly for a $500 per day tuna-fishing charter to be ruined because the cheap roller guides on your bargain-basement trolling rod didn't work, but this often happens.

Part of assembling a balanced fishing outfit means picking a rod suited to the task. These chapters will help you to do just that.

Surf fishing is to saltwater angling what trout fishing is to freshwater. It is a one-man game from start to finish.

—Van Campen Heilner

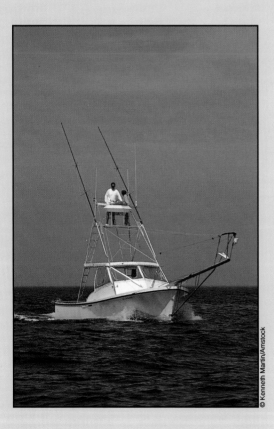

Chapter 4
Saltwater Spinning Rods

Modern saltwater spinning rods may range in length from 5 to 13 feet (1.5 to 4 m). Shorter rods are generally used for light-tackle casting for inshore species, while rods of 9 feet (2.7 m) and longer are commonly used for surf casting. In general, the shorter the rod is, the lighter the lure it's designed to cast—although this isn't a hard and fast rule. It's important to remember that any given rod is designed to perform best with a lure of a specific weight. When lighter or heavier lures are used, casting performance is diminished.

Most manufacturers put a label on the rod butt near the grip that specifies an appropriate lure-weight range as well as a line-size range. Remember that one specific weight will work best, so these lure-weight ranges are a compromise. You can also find this information at your local tackle shop and in most mail-order catalogs. For example, a 6½-foot (2-m), two-piece spinning rod classified by the maker as "light" indicates that the rod should be used with 2- to 6-pound-test (.9- to 2.7-kg-test) line for lures weighing ⅛ to ½ ounce (3.5 to 14 g). Unfortunately, these specifications can be very misleading, and you'll have to be very careful when selecting a rod on the basis of such labels. It is impossible to build a spinning rod that will cast ⅛- and ½-ounce (3.5- and 14-g) lures equally well (in spite of this particular maker's claim); and while 2- to 6-pound-test (.9- to 2.7-kg-test) line might be fine for ⅛-ounce (3.5-g) lures, such lines are impractical for ½-ounce (14-g) lures.

These surf-spinning rods are set up and ready in case a school of fish moves inshore.

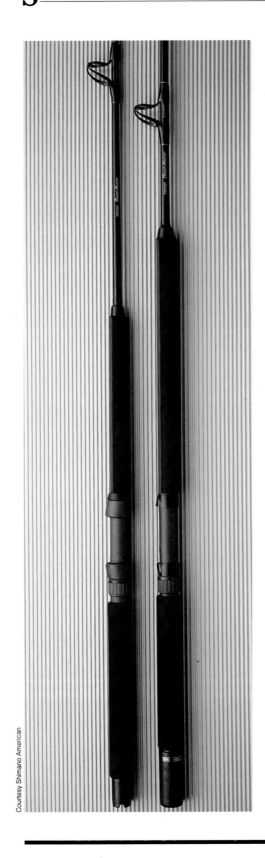

If possible, test-cast a rod before you buy it to make sure it fits your desired lure-weight range.

The best possible solution is to take your own spinning reel filled with your preferred line and a practice weight to your tackle shop, and talk the proprietor into letting you test-cast several rods. You'll immediately find which rods are best suited to the rest of your tackle, your casting style, and your particular method of fishing. If I find a rod I especially like by this method, I usually buy two of them in case one is eventually broken or the manufacturer discontinues that model. (If you own neither rod nor reel, describing the type of fishing you plan to do to a knowledgeable salesperson should help you select an appropriate outfit.)

Many people—mail-order customers, for example—won't be able to do this, however, and the next best approach is an educated reading of the rod's label. If a range of lure weights is specified, the narrowest range is likely to be the most accurate. In the previous example, there's a 400 percent difference between the ⅛-ounce (3.5-g) and ½-ounce (14-g) lures specified, which is too much. A range of ⅛ to ¼ ounce (3.5 to 7 g) is more realistic, as is any range with a span of no more than ¼ ounce (7 g).

If the range specified on the rod or in the catalog is a wide one—say ¼ to ⅝ ounce (7 to 17.5 g)—it's generally a safe bet that the middle to upper portion of that range will bring optimum performance from that particular rod. Note that this discussion has been based on lure weight and *not* line size. Lure weight

BLUEFISH

Bluefish are perhaps the most commonly sought light-tackle game fish along North America's Atlantic Coast, especially in recent years when populations of striped bass and northern weakfish have been in decline. These fish are common from Massachusetts to Florida in season, and recent years of warm weather have produced exceptional bluefishing in southeastern Maine as bluefish have followed migrating schools of menhaden—a favored food—northward. Blues may range in weight from young-of-the-year snappers at a few ounces to a maximum recorded weight of about 45 pounds (20 kg). The rod-and-reel record, set in North Carolina, stands at slightly over 30 pounds (13.6 kg), and any bluefish over 20 pounds (9 kg) has been exceptional in recent seasons. Top months for bluefishing are June through mid-October from Massachusetts to New Jersey; April and November are best around Cape Hatteras, North Carolina; while December and March are often the best months for bluefish along the Florida coast. Unfortunately, there are none to be found in Canada.

Bluefish can be exceptionally voracious and will sometimes eat or strike at almost any lure or bait. At other times, the fish may seem dour and suspicious, and it can be difficult to get a strike. Small ⅛-ounce (3.5-g) Kastmaster spoons work well for little snappers, as do small streamer flies or live minnows. Surf-casters and boat anglers use larger spoons and swimming plugs in casting or trolling for larger bluefish, while surface plugs, such as Pencil Poppers, sometimes elicit smashing strikes. Bait anglers usually use chunks of mackerel or menhaden on the bottom, depending on which baitfish is prevalent in the area to be fished. Bluefish have exceptionally sharp teeth and will try deliberately to bite the unwary angler trying to remove a hook. These teeth sometimes make necessary the use of a wire leader ahead of one's bait or lure, since the bluefish may otherwise simply cut the line on the strike.

is what bends the rod in casting and is independent of line weight in considering rod selection. Using the correct line weight is simple common sense: Heavy line goes with heavy rods and lures, and vice versa.

Spinning rods are uniquely characterized by fairly large diameter line guides that form a rapidly decreasing cone when viewed from butt to rod tip. The design of fixed-spool spinning reels is such that in casting, the line comes off the reel in large open spirals that slap against the rod blank, which creates friction and diminishes the cast. The large guides on a spinning rod are designed to capture the wide line spirals and quickly reduce them to a straight-line motion for maximum casting efficiency. Guides, of course, also distribute the tension along the rod's length, so it bends evenly when casting or fighting fish. As such, the guides must be properly spaced on the rod.

Almost all spinning-rod guides are now of premium makes, so guide quality needn't be an object of great concern as long as you're dealing with a major-brand rod. The guides will be made of hardened metal or hardened metal with super-hard ceramic inserts to prevent line wear. You should check periodically to make sure the guide inserts haven't been cracked by a sharp blow, and that the metal guides are likewise undamaged. In either case the guide may start to fray and weaken your line, or it may fail totally, which could cause a concentration of bending stress and thus break your rod.

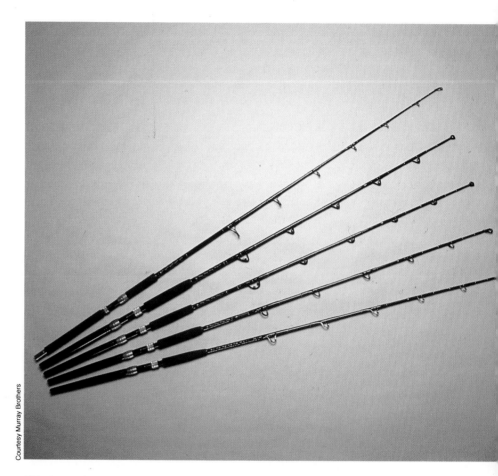

Courtesy Murray Brothers

Most rods come in a range of sizes and weights, and a particular model must be matched to the rest of your tackle.

Reelseats on spinning rods are either of the fixed (screw-locking) or sliding-band variety. If you have a screw-locking seat, you only have to check periodically while fishing to make sure the locking ring has remained tight. This is especially important after the outfit has been transported in a car or boat with the reel mounted, since the vibrations of a motor will tend to loosen the reelseat. It's very disconcerting to have the reel come off the rod while you're casting or playing a fish. It's even more silly (when it happens) than it sounds, but it can happen.

Rods with sliding-band reelseats are usually of ultralight variety in which the reelseat is subject to the least stress. Many people don't consider ultralight spinning in salt water, but this light gear offers superb sport with all sorts of inshore species—from small flounder and bluefish to small bonefish, ladyfish, and snapper. Use the sliding rings on either side of the reel foot to clamp the reel to the rod grip slightly forward of center. If my reel is to be left on the rod for an extended period, I use electrician's tape to keep the bands from working loose, as they tend to do with time and use.

Graphite fiber, either as a primary component or in combination with fiberglass, is the basis for most modern spinning rods. These rods are typically tip-action rods in most designs. They evolved from the needs of freshwater bass anglers who needed a light tip to cast small lures and a powerful butt section to facilitate hook setting and playing largemouths in heavy cover. (There are tip-action fiberglass rods, but they are very unusual: Most graphite rods, however, are tip

action.) Usually, the greater the percentage of graphite in a rod's composition, the more expensive the rod will be. Fiberglass rods are usually at the low end of the price range, but shouldn't be neglected as they do offer some advantages. Other features being equal, fiberglass flexes more easily than graphite. These more easily bending or "softer" rods are a big plus in casting ultralight lures and baits that are just too light to bend a stiffer graphite model. Also, the quicker casting stroke demanded by stiffer graphite models can snap natural baits such as worms or minnows right off the hook. This is an important consideration in surf casting, where a fast-actioned graphite rod will give more distance with artificial lures but can be frustrating to use with bait. A more deeply flexing fiberglass or composite rod is usually the most desirable for fishing natural baits in the surf.

Day in and day out, spinning rods are the most common of all saltwater rods because they are the most versatile. They are also more widely available than other rod types, and are found everywhere from coastal hardware stores to specialized fishing tackle shops. If you remember nothing else, remember to match the size of your spinning rod to the rest of your tackle and to the size of the fish you expect to catch. As ever, balanced tackle is the key to successful angling.

*Tarpon fishing by night is exciting work,
somewhat too exciting for many people.*
— J. Turner-Turner (1902)

Chapter 5

Conventional Casting Rods

Saltwater casting rods for use with conventional reels are usually one of three types: light bait-casting, popping, and long surf-casting rods. Medium-weight freshwater tackle, such as that used for bass and pike, can be used in light-tackle saltwater casting for smaller species such as school striped bass or southern seatrout, as long as you remember to carefully use fresh water to rinse the corrosive salt from your tackle after each use.

Light bait-casting rods for inshore saltwater use may range from 5 to 7 feet (1.5 to 2.1 m) long, rated for 8- to 12-pound-test (3.6- to 5.4-kg-test) line, and lure weights of ¼ to ⅝ ounce (7 to 10 g). Lures or baits heavier than this are difficult to cast with single-handed rods and should be used with the two-handed versions described later in the chapter. Light bait-casting rods are characterized by a distinctive trigger-type reelseat and relatively small line guides. The trigger isn't related to shooting in any way; it's held by the index finger of the casting hand and is a substantial help in supporting the rod during the casting motion. Because bait-casting reels must be manipulated with the thumb while casting, these single-handed rods often feature offset reelseats that put the reel closer to the thumb, while still allowing a reasonable one-handed grip.

Two-handed, or popping, rods have a longer rear grip for two-handed support in casting heavier lures and usually have straight grips. It's worth noting that the bent rear grips on many single-handed bait-casting rods won't fit in rod holders mounted on many boats for trolling. If you're planning to troll as well as cast with your rod, check for fit first.

Guides on bait-casting rods can be relatively small since line comes off a bait-casting reel in a straight line when casting. Check your guides periodically for cracks or breaks that could wear the line or cause the guide to fail. One old trick worth mentioning is to slip a piece of nylon stocking or pantyhose through the guides, where you can use the sensitive material to feel any nicks or cracks.

Graphite-fiber rods and professional bass tournaments had both become widely popular by the mid-1970s; at least partly as a result, modern bait-casting rods have the stiff actions preferred by many bass anglers. This means that the lure accelerates very rapidly during the casting stroke and requires a skilled thumb on the revolving spool to avoid backlashes. Fiberglass and some fiberglass/graphite composite rods may have softer, deeper-flexing actions and are much easier to cast with lures of the appropriate weight. If you're buying your first bait-casting rod, ask the tackle salesperson for the softest action rod for your desired lure weight. This will make learning to cast much easier.

Single-handed bait-casting rods vary widely in length, action, and proper lure-weight capacity. For simplicity's sake, I'll call them ultralight, light, medium, and heavy. The distinction is based on the appropriate lure weights (and corresponding line weights) for each. Ultralight bait-casting rods are designed for lures of ⅛ to ¼ ounce (3.5 to 7 g). These might be used with 4-, 6-, or 8-pound-test (1.8-, 2.7-, or 3.6-kg-test) line, and should be of a softer action to facilitate use with very light lures. When using such light line on bait-casting reels, be very careful to keep it from slipping between the spool's edge and the reel frame. Light rods are fun to use for inshore fishing and on small saltwater species such as small striped bass, snapper bluefish, seatrout, ladyfish, and surf perch.

Light bait-casting rods are usually used with line testing at 6 to 10 pounds (2.7 to 4.5 kg) and lure weights of ¼ to ⅜ ounce (7 to 10 g) or slightly more. Assuming a reel of sufficient capacity (at least 200 yards [183 meters] of line), these rods can be great fun for bonefish that are often caught on spinning tackle in the same general size range.

Medium bait-casting rods accommodate lure weights from ⅜ to ⅝ ounce (10 to 17 g) using lines of 10- to 20-pound-test (4.5- to 9-kg-test). Such rods may be either single- or two-handed affairs and are commonly used for larger inshore species such as small bluefish or snook.

Heavy bait-casting rods for saltwater use are almost always two-handed rods carrying lures of ¾ to 1¼ ounces (21 to 35 g) or more. These are commonly called popping rods in many areas and are the most versatile of all saltwater casting rods. They are light

Landing a Hawaiian blue marlin.

***A native Hawaiian fisherman
after small tuna.***

enough to provide some sport with smaller seatrout, snook, or redfish, for example, yet heavy enough to handle heavier, stronger fish such as tarpon, large striped bass, or bluefish. Medium bait-casting rods usually have a two-handed rear grip about 18 inches (45 cm) long that allows the angler to use both hands in casting heavier lures. In retrieving lures and fighting fish, the rod butt can be braced

against the abdomen, and the left hand used on the short foregrip ahead of the reel while cranking with the right hand. These rods usually range in length from 7 to 9 feet (2.1 to 2.7 m). Shorter versions are most appropriate for casting from a boat. I use a 9-footer for surf-casting as long as the wind is down and the waves aren't too high.

Conventional surf-casting tackle is preferable to heavy spinning gear when extreme casting distances are necessary, in bait fishing, and whenever heavy line must be used to

© Tim Choate

Protection from the sun is essential for anyone planning a long day on open water.

and rear grip to facilitate a powerful two-handed cast. One-piece rods, even in extreme lengths, are preferred for this type of fishing, although they must generally be transported on the roof rack of a car. Two-piece versions are fairly common, but the severe stresses of heavy-lure casting will often cause the ferrule or rod joint to twist, causing a misalignment of the butt and tip sections that must be periodically corrected by taking the rod apart and putting it together again.

Fiberglass or fiberglass/graphite composite rods are usually better for casting a heavy sinker and natural bait because they allow the rod to accelerate more slowly during the casting stroke. All-graphite models tend to be very stiff and can cause soft baits to snap off the hook during casting. The same rods, however, may be better than fiberglass for casting artificial lures, since the rod's rapid acceleration in casting will allow some lures to be cast farther.

Conventional casting rods are specialized tools, usually used by more experienced anglers in a wide range of situations, each one of which might require a different and specific rod model. When used in conjunction with conventional casting reels (page 28), these rods enable you to cast longer distances in some situations and allow better control than other tackle types when fighting strong, heavy fish.

handle big fish around obstructions such as rocks in the water. Surf-casting rods may range from 9 to 13 feet (2.7 to 4 m) long and usually feature a split grip. In this case, the reelseat and foregrip are located 20 to 30 inches (51 to 76 cm) ahead of the rod butt

RED DRUM

Also called channel bass or redfish, these popular game fish got the name "red drum" from their ability to create a drumming noise by vibrating a muscle against an internal, air-filled bladder. The largest drum (40 to 60 pounds [18 to 27 kg]) are usually taken in the fall and spring on North Carolina's Outer Banks. Smaller redfish are common in Florida and along the Gulf Coast, where they frequent shallow inshore waters such as Florida Bay and the Ten Thousand Islands area.

Redfish in the southern part of their range may reach 10 pounds or more, but 3- to 6-pound (1.3- to 2.7-kg) fish are the most common. Fly, plug, and spinning tackle are all commonly used for these fish in Florida and the
Gulf states, as the redfish will usually hit streamer flies, jigs, or small swimming plugs. It can be exciting fishing, as the fish are often spotted feeding in shallow water as the angler cruises quietly along in a shallow-draft skiff. Fishing for the giant drum of the Outer Banks requires heavy surf-casting gear capable of handling 4- to 6-ounce (113- to 169-g) lead sinkers and a large chunk of fresh mullet or other bait. Even the large drum here will sometimes take artificials such as large Hopkins spoons cast from shore, or even a big streamer fly if the fish can be reached by this method. Natural baits, however, are the most consistently productive methods for big channel bass in the surf.

This glorious fish made a leap of thirty feet at least, low and swift, which gave me time to gauge his enormous size and species...
— Zane Grey

Chapter 6
Boat, Trolling, and Stand-up Rods

Back in the days when Zane Grey, the famous author of such books as *Riders of the Purple Sage*, was building his fame writing novels and spending his fortune cruising the world's oceans in search of big-game fishes, offshore trolling rods were typically made of solid wood, such as hickory or laminated sections of bamboo. Today, even though graphite fiber dominates light-tackle rods, fiberglass is the norm for offshore rods because of its strength and resiliency. From the simplest boat rods used in bottom fishing for flounder to the most sophisticated trolling rods for giant marlin, most contemporary rods of fiberglass offer high strength at a relatively low price.

None of the rods described in this chapter are designed for casting a lure or natural bait. If you're going to be bottom fishing from a boat, shore, bridge, or pier and will need to cast your bait, check the conventional or spinning rods described in the previous two chapters. The same is true for trolling rods, which are designed for trolling only.

As a simplest case, some rods are designed only for bottom fishing over the side of a boat or from a bridge. These rods are usually short—4 to 5 feet (1.2 to 1.5 m) long as an example—and since the bait is going to be dropped straight down, no real reach is necessary. These are almost always rods designed for conventional, revolving-spool reels. Guides will generally be small bridge guides as found on other conventional rods.

A selection of trolling tackle held by what offshore fisher-men call a "rocket launcher."

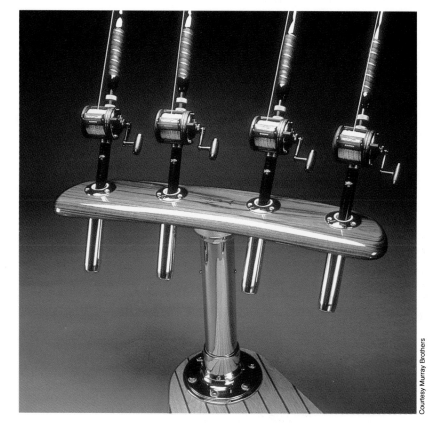

Courtesy Murray Brothers

As these simple rods are usually the most inexpensive, reelseats are typically low quality, but they should feature at least one screw-locking ring to hold the reel firmly. The rod butt may be 18 to 24 inches (46 to 61 cm) long for tucking under your arm or into a rod holder. I should add that I don't own or use any of these rods, because their uses are too limited. Instead, I use my conventional casting rods for bottom fishing, which give me the advantage of being able to cast instead of simply lowering the bait over the side. For the bottom angler on a budget, however, these rods are the least expensive way of getting into the game.

Trolling rods are a decidedly different matter. Saltwater trolling rods are usually designed specifically for trolling. Their actions and guide systems simply aren't conducive to good casting. Most of these rods are designed for specific line weights. The lightest of these—for 12-pound-test (5.4-kg-test) line—may have a special line guide at the tip called a roller guide. Just as the name implies, this guide features a little grooved wheel or roller over which the line travels, and which helps to reduce the friction stresses on both line and rod. Heavier rod models for line weights ranging up to 130-pound-test (59-kg-test) should have roller guides over their entire length.

Rod action for most rods is described in the rod's ability to cast a lure of a certain weight, but this thinking doesn't apply to trolling rods that aren't used for casting. The tips on most trolling rods are relatively flexible, designed to help absorb shock in fighting big fish. One way to gauge the action of a trolling rod is to be sure that the first 18 inches (45 cm) of the rod will bend through an arc of 90 degrees when a pull equal to one half of the rod's designated line weight is applied to the tip. Thus a 20-pound (9-kg) trolling rod—which doesn't weigh 20 pounds, but

© M. Timothy O'Keefe/Tom Stack & Associates

Boats like this sportfisherman are the most common in off-shore trolling areas.

is designed for 20-pound-test (9-kg-test) line—should have its tip bent over at 90 degrees under a 10-pound (4.5-kg) pull.

The remainder of the trolling rod's action is quite stiff, although the entire rod should assume a slight curve with a hard pull on the line. The butt and midsection of the rod, however, function as the angler's lever in working against the fish and must be stiff enough to stand severe strain. There's usually 18 to 24

inches (46 to 61 cm) of butt behind the reel-seat on these rods, the end of which is often slotted to mate with a gimbal socket in the center of a fighting chair at the rear of the boat. Or, the rod butt can be placed in a socket on a special belt worn by the angler when fighting a fish.

The reelseat and other components must be of top quality to avoid failure when fighting big fish. The stresses placed on tackle by a marlin weighing half a ton (453 kg) or more can't be overemphasized. Many quality troll-

BLACK MARLIN

Although both the black and closely related blue marlin have the potential to reach more than 2,000 pounds (906 kg), the black marlin has remained for many years as the largest rod-and-reel catch at slightly more than 1,500 pounds (676 kg). Every year a few hundred anglers make the long trek to Cairns, Australia, to troll the waters of the Great Barrier Reef and other nearby spots commonly regarded as the best places to catch a "grander," as blacks over 1,000 pounds (453 kg) are called. It is some of the most exotic, exhausting, and expensive fishing in the world, as one can easily spend more than $1,000 per day in charter and other costs for the mere chance of catching a giant black—and there are absolutely no guarantees of success.

Tackle for these fish is commonly in the 130-pound (59-kg) trolling class, the heaviest available, and features a large trolling reel spooled with half a mile or more of line. After taking a trolled bait, the fish may expend much of its energy in wild leaps, in which case the fight may be a relatively few backbreaking hours. If the fish goes deep and runs rather than leaps, the fight may take a dozen backbreaking hours or even longer. Anglers have been known to give up in exhaustion, cutting the line after despairing of ever landing the fish. Smaller black marlin, in the 200- to 400-pound (91- to 181-kg) range, are sometimes common along the Pacific coast of Panama, where they can provide grand sport on 20- to 50-pound (9- to 22.6-kg) tackle.

Several lures or baits are usually trolled simultaneously for billfish or tuna.

ing reels have a threaded, D-shaped strap that is used in addition to the reelseat rings to lock the reel on the rod. There may also be harness lugs on top of the reel allowing the angler to use a kidney or shoulder harness in fighting a big fish.

Stand-up fishing has become increasingly popular with many offshore anglers in recent years. This simply means fighting a large fish on trolling tackle while standing up, without the use of a fighting chair. Rods for this kind of fishing are generally similar to heavy-duty trolling rods but feature a shorter butt and longer grip ahead of the reelseat. This allows the reel handles to be comfortably close to the body and also allows both hands to be used well above the reel in pulling for maximum leverage. These rods may have either slotted or simple capped rod butts, but in either case must be used with a special belt into which the rod butt is placed for maximum support. Some stand-up anglers also use a waist belt attached to the reel for more leverage, but this makes me nervous. With bigger fish and heavy line, there's a real risk of the angler being yanked over the side of a boat before the harness can be released!

Stand-up fishing may be the most sporting method of offshore fishing, since it places a greater premium on the angler's fish-fighting skill. Many anglers fish in this manner for small- to medium-size tuna and yellowtail, for example, and a few even seek giant marlin with stand-up tackle.

© Philip Rosenberg

With a fly rod the number of fish which may be caught is purely a question of physical endurance.

—A. W. Dimock (1890)

Chapter 7
Fly Rods

Like most rods, a fly rod is designed to cast a very specific weight. Since saltwater flies are essentially weightless, the weight being thrown is that of the bulky line, which is cast in a long, unrolling loop to deliver the fly. A difference between fly and other rods is that the casting weight—the line—isn't measured in ounces, but rather according to a standardized system adopted by the American Fishing Tackle Manufacturer's Association (AFTMA) in 1961 (and used worldwide) that designates fly-line sizes from 1 through 14, with the latter being heaviest. Thus, fly rods are referred to as a "1 weight" or a "6 weight" and so forth, depending on what size line the particular rod is designed to cast. For saltwa-ter fly fishing, the most commonly used sizes are 8-weight and heavier, although lighter, trout-size tackle is appropriate for smaller saltwater species as long as the wind isn't blowing so hard that casting a lightweight line becomes impossible.

With fly rods, the designated line weight is almost totally independent of rod length and depends mostly on a particular manufactur-er's design. One rod maker offers a 9-foot (2.7-m), 4-weight for small dry flies on a large trout river. The very same maker may have a 9-foot (2.7-m), 14-weight whose stiffness makes it a specialty tool for casting to ocean-going marlin that have been teased to within casting range from the back of a boat. For most saltwater fly fishing, the rods you'll encounter will be from 8½ to 9½ feet (2.5 to 2.7 m) long, taking lines from an 8-weight, which is useful for bonefish, small redfish, and smaller striped bass, up to a robust 12-weight that might be used for big stripers, bluefish, and even sailfish and marlin.

This angler is leaning into a fly-hooked bonefish.

Most beginning saltwater fly anglers are in areas where they'll be fishing in sheltered bays or estuaries for bonefish, redfish, or small jacks or smaller striped bass and bluefish. The best fly rod for starters will be a 9-foot (2.7-m) rod for a 9-weight line. This rod is light enough for even a small bonefish or striper to give a good account of itself and is capable of allowing you to handle larger fish that you may encounter. Many people make the mistake of starting a beginner with a rod that's too light, too short, or both, which is more difficult to cast in the inevitable wind and only leads to frustration.

It is absolutely essential that the fly-casting outfit be balanced; that is, the line and rod must match as to line-size designation. The only exception is in the case of a novice who's having trouble getting the feel of the line in the air while casting. In this case it may be advisable to use one line size larger, effectively overloading the rod and providing a greater feel. After some casting proficiency is gained, the switch back to the correct line can be made. Most major fly-tackle makers offer balanced outfits that include a matched rod, reel, and line at the very least. These are usually less expensive than the individual components purchased separately.

Most premium fly-rod grips are made of glued and shaped cork rings with the reelseat located behind the grip. The reel is usually fastened with a threaded ring to the reelseat. Some freshwater models have a reelseat

based on sliding bands, but these aren't strong enough for saltwater use. There may be a small hook-keeper ring located on the rod butt just forward of the grip. This is for storing your fly and isn't a line guide; many

© Tony Mandile

The large, rounded butt on this saltwater fly rod can be pressed comfortably into your abdomen when fighting large fish.

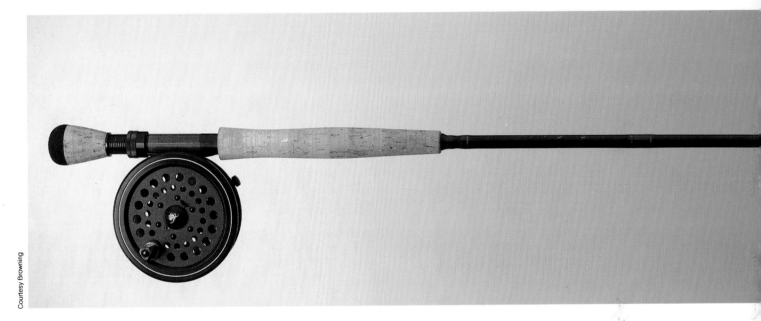

Courtesy Browning

first-timers make the mistake of stringing their line here. The larger and first guide on the butt section is known as the stripping guide. It is this guide that gets most of the wear as you strip or reel in line. Check to make sure it isn't cracked or rough in any way. The remainder of the guides are usually snake guides, so called because of their twisted-wire design. The last or tip guide is usually pear shaped and may feature a ceramic insert. Many saltwater fly rods have oversize guides, which can be a big plus if a strong fish suddenly takes off and your line is a little tangled. Hopefully—and this isn't always true — the tangle will pass freely through the larger guides and allow you to keep fighting the fish. If it doesn't, it's likely

that the running fish will break the rod or at least tear off the line guides. In either case, it's a disaster. Obviously, the best answer is to keep your line tangle free in the first place.

Most fly rods are of at least a two-piece design and some may be three, four, or even more pieces for easier storage and travel. Ferrules in these cases are usually of the sleeve or spigot variety. Sleeve-type ferrules fit one end of a section over the end of the preceding section. If stuck, they can be loosened with a gentle twisting. Spigot ferrules rely on a round tube that fits inside the mating sections and is permanently fixed inside one of them. Spigot ferrules can be more easily damaged by twisting and should be parted with a straight pull only. In either case, keep your

BONEFISH

These powerful, silver fish may be the ultimate challenge for light-tackle saltwater anglers. A hooked bonefish can accelerate to nearly 30 miles an hour on its initial shallow-water run, which may extend for 200 yards (183 m) or more before the fish stops and allows you to regain some line. Excellent bonefishing can be found from Florida's Biscayne Bay south through the Florida Keys and Bahamas to the Atlantic coast of Mexico, notably in southern Yucatán. Florida and Bahamian bonefish may average 3 to 6 pounds (2.7 kg), with a 30-inch-(76-cm) long, 10-pound (4.5-kg) fish a fair possibility. Mexican bonefish tend to be more numerous, but are smaller on the average—usually around 2 pounds (1 kg).

Bonefish cruise over shallow tidal flats searching for small crabs, shrimp, and other food. Their silver color makes them hard to see in the water, and the fish are easily spooked by a poorly aimed cast or an angler who approaches too closely. Use polarized glasses to help your vision when wading or fishing from a slowly moving boat. Keeping the sun at your back will also help you to see more fish by minimizing glare on the water's surface. Medium-weight spinning tackle with at least 200 yards (183 m) of 8- to 10-pound-test (3.6- to 4.5-kg-test) line is ideal together with a small (⅛- to ¼-ounce [3.5- to 7-g]) bonefish jig, of which the best known is a Wiggle Jig. Fly anglers should start with a 9-foot (2.7-m), 9-weight graphite rod with a weight-forward floating line, at least 200 yards (183 m) of backing line, a leader tapered to a 10-pound-test (4.5-kg-test) tip, and an assortment of bonefish flies in sizes 4, 6, and 8. Crazy Charlies and Bonefish Specials are basic fly patterns. You'll be casting to cruising fish as you spot them, and you must be able to cast quickly and accurately a few feet in front of the moving fish without scaring it.

*Here is a basic set-up for salt-
water fly fishing.*

© Tim Choate

ferrules wiped clean and lightly lubricate them with paraffin if need be.

To go beyond the beginner's outfit I described earlier in this chapter, you'll need to know how to match your rod/line size to the kinds of fish you're trying to catch. Just as a rod is designed to cast a certain size line, so the combination is most effective in casting flies of a certain size. A large, air-resistant tarpon fly, for example, is very hard to cast on a light 8-weight outfit because the line's mass is insufficient to carry the big fly through the air. And while you could cast a small bonefish fly with a 12-weight tarpon outfit, you'd lose some of the delicacy that's essential for spooky bonefish.

Eight- and 9-weight rods are middleweights, suitable for flies to size 2/0 (page 103) and smaller. Remember that the lighter the line, the more difficult it will be to cast in the wind and choose your rod size accordingly. Eight-weight rods, especially, are best in situations where there's little wind. If you're consistently fishing with small flies, these are the rods of choice.

Ten-, 11-, and 12-weight rods are the intermediate heavyweights and are the most versatile sizes. Ten-weights are probably the largest practical size for tropical-flats species such as bonefish and permit, yet are strong enough to handle tarpon to 100 pounds (45 kg) or so. Larger rods in this range are best for larger fish such as tarpon to 200 pounds (90 kg) and jumbo striped bass. Many rods

in this size range are extremely stiff and powerful, designed more for fish fighting than for casting. Others of the same line-weight designation are more flexible, allowing easier casting at the expense of fish-pulling power. Test-cast some heavy rods at your dealer's shop and make your choice depending on the kind of fishing you'll be doing. If you're after big tarpon, you won't be casting that often and a really stiff rod is okay. But if you're going after giant striped bass, you'll be making many, many casts, and a softer rod will make this job easier.

Thirteen- and 14-weight rods are real specialty tools and most saltwater fly anglers will never even pick one up. Rods of this caliber

Small boats are ideal for salt-water fly rodding in protected waters.

© Kenneth Martin/Amstock

offshore species. Typical sailfish fly fishing, for example, means that the fish is teased with a special bait right up behind a moving boat. When the fish is close and excited by the teaser, the teaser is yanked clear, the boat is put out of gear, and the fly-caster casts an immense streamer fly to the fish—all in the space of a few seconds. There may be no need to cast more than a dozen times in the course of a day's fishing by this method, so the rod is designed with a premium on fish-fighting power at the expense of casting characteristics, which are usually poor at best.

The art of fly-casting itself is superficially simple but requires hours of practice for reasonable proficiency. Teaching fly-casting is beyond the scope of this book, but here are a few suggestions. First, see if you can find a fly-fishing friend to teach you. There's no substitute for personal instruction to get you started, and you might consider attending one of the many fly-fishing schools held by both manufacturers and professional casting teachers. You can locate a school by checking the advertisements in one of several fly-fishing magazines you'll find on most good newsstands. Some fly-casting videotapes are available, as are books on the subject. Two highly recommended books, both by excellent teachers are: *Fly-Casting Techniques* by Joan Wulff (New York: Nick Lyons Books, 1987); and *The Essence of Flycasting* by Mel Krieger (Write to: Club Pacific, 790 27th Avenue, San Francisco, CA 94121).

are usually designed for sailfish and marlin. The rods are exceptionally stiff, with great lifting power that's a help in fighting these

PART III
RIGS, LURES, and FLIES

Saltwater fishing can be as simple as dropping a baited hook over the side of a bridge or boat—but such simplicity is the exception. There are thousands upon thousands of different lures, flies, and fishing rigs to choose from. At first glance the choices may seem difficult; however, as with other tackle categories, these items vary according to a few basic principles. Understanding these concepts can simplify things considerably.

The term rigs includes the various combinations of hooks and sinkers (weights) used in bait fishing. As with most fishing methods, there are a few basic rules to follow, covered in the following chapters, that ultimately mean more fishing success with less lost or damaged tackle for any angler.

When you visit a saltwater tackle shop, you're apt to encounter racks containing hundreds of different saltwater lures. Making a random selection based on whim or a favorite color almost guarantees that you'll catch little or nothing. Using the selection criteria given in this section should narrow your choices down to a small handful based on the kind of fish you're after, where you'll be fishing, and what type of tackle you use.

The same general approach holds true for saltwater flies, a category that in the last ten years has grown enormously in popularity and variety. You won't, however, be using the same flies for bluefish as you will for bonefish, for example, so, again, the choices can be simplified using the criteria given in this section's chapter on saltwater fly patterns.

The Gulf Stream and the other great ocean currents are the last wild country there is left.
—Ernest Hemingway

Chapter 8
Basic Saltwater Lures

Just about any artificial lure you use in fresh water will work at one time or another for some saltwater species, but in general saltwater lures are both simpler and stronger than their freshwater counterparts. Spinners and spoons are staples of freshwater tackleboxes and are seldom used in salt water, for example, although large spoons are sometimes used for salmon in the Pacific Northwest. Most saltwater anglers, however, rely on an assortment of plugs and jigs in a wide variety of sizes, all of which must feature strong, corrosion-resistant hardware and hooks to withstand the rigors of saltwater fishing.

PLUGS

Plugs for saltwater use fall into four basic categories: poppers, surface skimmers, swimmers, and deep-divers. In cases where I expect to encounter large numbers of fish—schools of marauding bluefish, for example—I often replace the plug's treble hooks with Siwash-style single hooks to make unhooking and releasing fish easier. Often, too, I make the hooks on my plugs (whether single or treble) barbless by flattening the barbs with pliers. This also makes unhooking fish easier and faster. It's also safer, as anyone who has tried to land and unhook a big, thrashing striped bass with a mouthful of treble hooks after dark can attest. If the fish manages to slam a hook into my hand while I'm trying to land it, I can free myself from the barbless hook fairly easily. Having caught hundreds of saltwater fish on barbless-hook plugs, I've never lost a fish due to a lack of hook barbs. If anything, barbless hooks give better hook-setting penetration on the strike; and I heartily recommend them.

Popping plugs, as the name implies, are designed to pop and gurgle when yanked along the water's surface, making a disturbance that may often "call" fish from a considerable distance. This plug design features a concave or cupped face that creates the pop or splash when the plug is worked on the surface. Most are also tail weighted, which means that the weight of the plug is concentrated toward the rear. This makes the plug fly straight without tumbling and tangling the line when a cast is made.

Surface-disturbing plugs generally have a more subtle action than poppers and are often more effective for that reason. These plugs skim or wobble along the water's surface in response to twitches and yanks made by the angler's rod tip. The Stan Gibbs' Pencil Popper (which is not really a popper) and the old Zara Spook are perhaps the best known of this plug type. Various saltwater species will respond best to different retrieves with this style plug. Jacks may require a fast, whipping-style retrieve, while striped bass sometimes respond best to a slower, teasing retrieve style. These plugs fish best on rods with flexible tips that permit the most action to be given to the lure.

© Philip Rosenberg

Jigs like these are the most common and basic of saltwater lures.

Likewise, swimming plugs do what their name implies: They swim with a rocking or wobbling motion just under the water's surface in imitation of various baitfishes. Common to these plugs is a dished face or wobbling plate at the head, which causes the lure to dive and wobble when retrieved. Weight distribution within these plugs is gen-

© Kenneth Martin/Amstock

This Atom Popper is a classic bluefish and striper lure.

erally even from head to tail, which means that they sometimes tumble in the air when cast and tangle in the line. Make sure you use a smooth, even casting stroke to minimize this problem. Swimming-plug size is widely variable, and the most useful plug sizes will depend on the size baitfish prevalent in your area.

Deep-diving plugs are typically swimming plugs with an extra-large lip or wobbling plate at the front. The large lip causes the plug to dive deeply with its wobbling action when cast or trolled, sometimes as deep as 20 feet (6 m) or more, depending on the model and size of the plug. These plugs are more commonly trolled than cast, but even the caster will find them useful for fishing a deep hole or cut where fish often congregate.

With all types of plugs, strength is an important consideration. Many smaller freshwater plugs are also used in salt water, but you may first want to switch the plug's hooks to stronger versions. Also, many freshwater plugs, especially smaller swimming plugs, are hollow plastic, and fish such as barracuda or

bluefish may simply bite them in half! Solid wood or plastic plugs are preferred for that reason. In any case, it's desirable to have what's called "through-wire" construction in your plugs, which means that all of the plug's hooks are connected to a strand of heavy wire that runs through the plug's body. This is the most fail-safe system for really tough fish, as this next story shows.

"It was incredible!" Charlie Bovey yelled at me from his car window as he stopped on his way home from the beach. "Look at this!" He was waving a big striped-bass plug in the air. I walked over to look at it; the hooks all were either smashed flat or bent straight.

"Did you run over this with your car, Charlie?" I asked him. "Car, nothin'! That was the biggest striper I ever saw. Hooked her just at daylight in that riptide by Swainson's Hole. Next thing you know, all I could feel was her mashing her jaw into the sand out there, trying to rub the plug out of her mouth. She rolled once on top — I saw her then. She was 50 pounds (22.5 kg) easy, and then she started banging the bottom again with my plug. I couldn't move her at all, and finally all I had was a dead slack line with this bent-up piece of garbage on it. What can you do?"

Charlie was almost in tears, and I asked him to wait while I went down into my basement and came back with some extra-strong Mustad treble hooks. I explained how he could attach them to any plug with stainless-

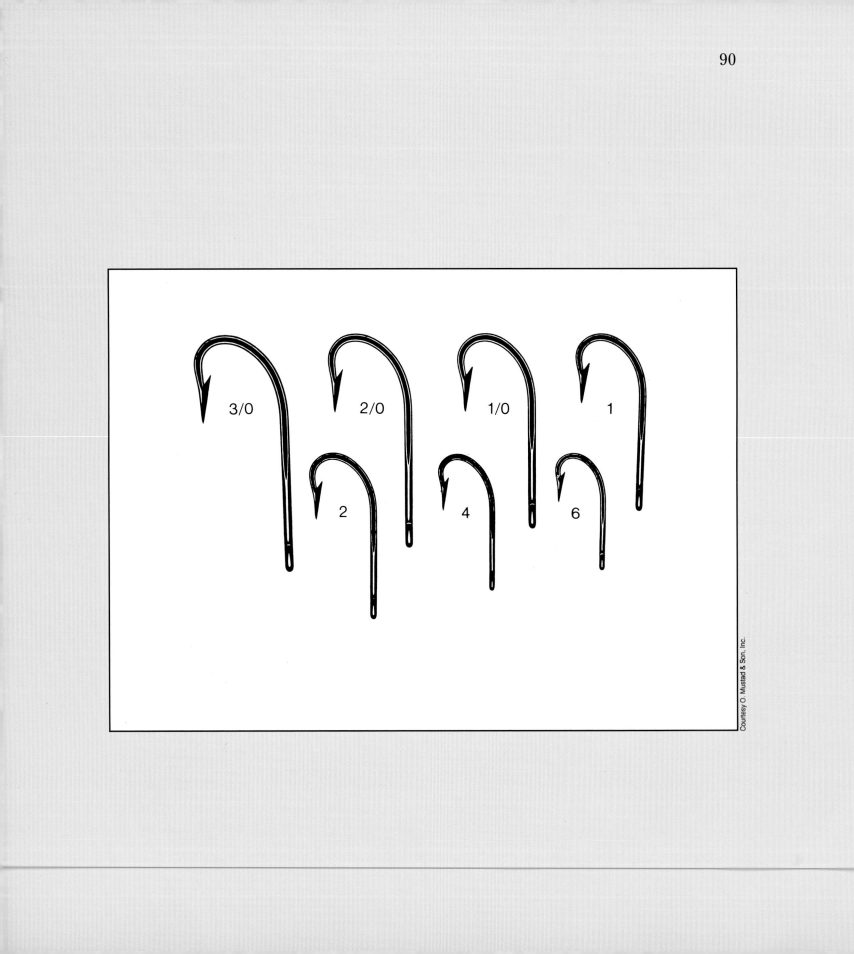

UNDERSTANDING HOOK SIZES

Hook sizes are often a confounding question for novice anglers, because the size numbers bear no relation to the actual size of a hook. The numbering system is archaic, and it is now just a matter of convention. Below is a simple way to help you understand the different hook sizes.

First, remember that a size-1 hook is the center point of a size scale. Hook sizes 2, 4, 6, 8, and so on to size 28 get smaller as the size number increases, with size 28 being the smallest. There are no odd-numbered sizes (no size 17, for example) in this sequence. Going in the other direction, hook sizes larger than size 1 are noted with a number, a slash, and a zero: 1/0, 2/0, 3/0, and so on up to giant 20/0 shark hooks. This sequence does include odd-numbered sizes.

Most common saltwater hooks follow this system, which applies to both single hooks and to the treble (three-pointed) hooks commonly found on fishing lures. A few single hooks are shown on the opposite page in their actual size to give you some idea of relative size scales. In terms of usage, hooks for artificial flies usually range from a size 5/0 for large sailfish flies to size 28 for the very smallest trout flies that are less than ¼ inch (6 mm) long. Bait anglers commonly use hook sizes 2, 4, 6, and 8, and follow the general rule of using smaller hooks for smaller fish and vice versa.

© Philip Rosenberg

steel split rings. Sometimes, I added, there was nothing you *could* do. The big fish can just beat you in a fight. He said that that didn't make him feel any better and left, still shaking his head.

JIGS AND TINS

Jigs are the most basic and often the most effective of all saltwater lures. They are also usually the least expensive. In their simplest form, a lead head is molded to the hook near the eye, behind which is attached a clump of trailing bucktail or other long hair. When cast and properly retrieved, the jig darts up and down through the water like a small baitfish.

These lures may range in size from tiny 1/32-ounce (.8-g) versions used on ultralight spinning gear up to 5- or 6-ounce (141- or

The Kastmasters (right) will cast farther and better than the regular spoons (left).

170-g), and even larger versions are used for jigging either in deep, fast tidal currents or else straight down in water that's 50 to 100 feet (15 to 30 m) deep or more. Some polished metal jigs used for cod may weigh 16 ounces (452 g) and even more, as the weight is necessary to allow adequate rod "feel" for the angler bouncing his lure up and down near the bottom of 200 feet (61 m) of water. The weight of such lures prohibits actual casting, and they are fished straight up and down only.

So-called tins were just that: a slim block of

© Kenneth Martin/Amstock

These Hopkins spoons are especially heavy in proportion to their surface area, which means it's easier to cast for distance.

tin (or lead) molded around a long-shanked hook. The tin could be scraped with a knife or rubbed with sand to make it shiny, and the lure was designed to be cast and then retrieved rapidly so that the shiny sides resembled a baitfish. Tins are seldom used these days, but their design concept of dense weight and long-range casting lives on in such modern lures as Kastmasters and Hopkins, which are really a kind of spoon, but are still called tins by a few old-timers. These lures are extremely heavy in proportion to their surface area, and they are typically solid

brass covered by a shiny chrome finish. They wobble slightly on a steady retrieve, resembling a baitfish, and cast extremely well into a stiff head wind. When maximum casting distance, tough head winds, or both are the order of the day, these are the lures of choice.

PLASTIC LURES

Like their freshwater counterparts, soft plastic lures of assorted designs have become increasingly popular among saltwater anglers in the past twenty years. Most of these are fished with a standard jig head. Their general lack of durability–many are torn up after a fish or two–is more than offset by their low price. They are usually less expensive than live, natural baits and are often more effective.

The most common type of lure is a curly-

This is a typical swimming plug.

These offshore-trolling lures are made of molded plastic.

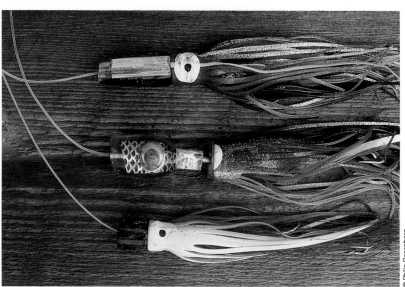

tailed grub that may range from 2 inches (5 cm) long for use on ultralight jigs up to 6 inches (15 cm) or so for jig heads weighing an ounce (28 g) or more. The molded curl in the soft-plastic tail has a built-in wiggling action when drawn through the water, and a wide variety of game fish find this irresistible. I've used these lures with great success on everything from bonefish and permit to striped bass. As a bonus, these lures will often take bottom fish such as flounder and fluke that are usually only caught on bait. For me, the most productive grub colors have been chartreuse, black, and white—in that order. Grubs of these colors are the closest thing I've ever

encountered to a universal, light-tackle saltwater lure.

Other plastic baits can be effective, too, although I've yet to find any with the grub's seemingly universal application. Large plastic worms are often effective on a jig head for striped bass and weakfish, and also for redfish (drum) and sea trout. In these cases my most frequent successes have been with a translucent red worm 6 to 8 inches (15 to 20 cm) long.

SPECIALTY LURES

Beyond the usual assortment of plugs, jigs,

Offshore-trolling lures are often more effective than natural baits.

This is the widely effective Pencil Popper.

Courtesy Murray Brothers

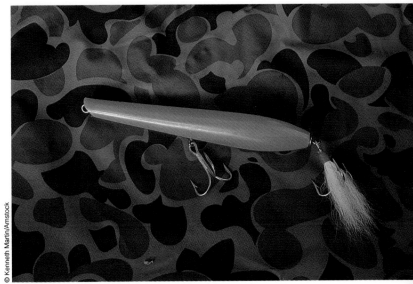

© Kenneth Martin/Amstock

and tins encountered by most light-tackle saltwater anglers is a whole world of specialty lures usually used in connection with large offshore fishes such as tuna and marlin. Blue-water trolling lures of the past were usually simple: often no more than a bunch of white feathers attached to a chromed head (called a "feather") or a frayed piece of white rope with a hook attached. The old standards still work, but now there are special molded offshore lures in a rainbow of colors and sizes and designed for different trolling speeds and even for specific fish species.

I'm not going to describe these at length because if you do charter an offshore fishing

trip, the skipper will show you how the lures are used. The general idea is a colorful skirt undulating behind a molded trolling head that features large eyes. The action when trolled at high speed varies with the lure, but one common design concept is to have holes drilled in the lure head. When trolled, these holes throw a violent pattern of spray or air bubbles to attract such fish as marlin or wahoo. In this era when catch-and-release fishing is good fishing conservation and good manners, offshore trolling lures allow the release of more uninjured fish than those taken with natural baits, which are more deeply swallowed on the strike.

All fish are difficult to take if you go about it in the wrong way.

—Burr Smidt

Chapter 9
Rigs

The general term "rigs" refers to various ways of connecting terminal tackle—hooks, swivels, sinkers, and so forth—to accommodate specific fishing situations. These are the nuances of saltwater fishing that can make the difference between catching fish or catching nothing. As just one example, using a common bank sinker with its rounded profile to hold your bait in a tidal current on a sandy bottom is almost useless, since the rounded sinker will just roll in the current. You'll catch more fish using a sharp-cornered pyramid sinker, the edges of which will dig into the sand and hold your bait in the right spot. Bank sinkers, however, work well on a rocky bottom where the rounded profile is less likely to become permanently lodged in the rocks.

When fishing with lures in areas of sharp rocks or coral, it's fairly common for monofilament line to become nicked or abraded near the lure, either when fighting a fish or in retrieving the lure over some obstruction. This means that the line will be substantially weakened and may snap the next time you hook a fish. You can at least partly avoid this problem by using a short leader of stronger line next to your lure. As an example, assume you're using 12-pound-test (5.4-kg-test) mono on a spinning outfit. Use a 24-inch (61-cm) section of 30-pound-test (13.6-kg-test) next to your lure. Instead of connecting your line to the leader with a blood knot—a common and very unreliable method—tie your line and leader to either end of a barrel swivel with a Trilene®Knot (page 123), which will be much stronger. When you cast, make sure the swivel is hanging just outside the tip guide. Casting will be slightly more difficult with the entire leader hanging outside the rod guides, but in a day's fishing you'll save yourself many dollars in lost lures by this method.

Lure anglers in salt water often find fish feeding on very small baitfish, much smaller than can be imitated by heavy, easy-to-cast lures. In this case, you can use what's called a dropper ahead of your lure. Using the same heavy leader and barrel swivel as in the previous example, use a Trilene®Knot to tie in a short (about 8 inches [20 cm]) length of heavy line (20- to 30-pound-test [9- to 13.5-kg-test]) to the barrel swivel so that the dropper connection extends at right angles to the main line and leader. Now attach a small streamer fly or plastic grub on an unweighted hook to the dropper line (again with a Trilene® Knot). Casting the heavy lure will enable you to reach the feeding fish, which will in all likelihood strike the small dropper. Many striped-bass anglers have found, for example, that a streamer-fly dropper ahead of a large plug will often outfish the plug itself by a factor of five to one or even more.

When bottom fishing with a sinker and natural bait, there's one general principle that applies whether you're fishing from a bridge, pier, or boat. Rig your sinker and bait hook or hooks so that the sinker doesn't diminish your ability to detect a subtle bite. This usually, but not always, means tying the bait hooks to the line above the sinker with the kind of dropper arrangement that's described above.

The right terminal rig is essential for the surf fisherman.

Another valuable bottom-fishing technique is called a "fish-finder" rig. This method allows the fish to pick up the bait without encountering the sinker's weight and still allows you to have a sensitive feel on the line. To create a fish-finder rig, slide the line through the eye of the sinker before attaching the barrel swivel, leader, and hook. When the sinker and bait are resting on the bottom, a biting fish can draw the line freely through the sinker's eye without feeling the weight of the sinker, which could cause him to drop the bait. This assumes that the sinker eye is small enough that the barrel swivel can't slip back through. If it does, the advantage is lost and you'll need a larger swivel.

A spreader is a device commonly used by flounder anglers. It consists of a straight piece of heavy wire with a loop in the middle and a loop at each end. A short leader with hook attached is placed on each end of the spreader. The line and sinker are then attached to the middle. Obviously, this device lets you haul in two fish at once when the bite is on. And there's one more little trick that can make this rig much more effective, which I learned courtesy of Eric Spicer during our last flounder expedition.

The thin April sunlight was almost warm as we anchored our small skiff in the middle of a Massachusetts harbor. We each rigged up a medium-weight spinning outfit with spreader rigs, sinkers, and hooks baited with small pieces of sea worm. Lowering these to the bottom over the side of the boat, we started the routine of gently lifting and dropping the rigs to the bottom, expecting that the puffs of mud created would attract some

flounder. After an hour or so we each had some flounder in the bucket, but Eric had been catching two to my one. Since we were using identical rigs—or so I thought—it was a puzzle.

"Okay," I finally said. "It's time to fess up! What are you doing that I'm not?"

Eric smiled while reeling in yet another flounder. I finally noticed that his lead sinker was painted bright orange, while mine was a conventional dull gray. "Sometimes I use a bright yellow one instead of orange," he laughed. "It can really make a difference. I don't know why, but the color seems to attract more flounder to the bait."

There are, as you may have inferred from these few examples, hundreds of ways of rigging your terminal tackle to meet a specific need. At the other end of the spectrum from the bridge and pier bottom anglers are the offshore specialists seeking marlin, sailfish, and tuna, and dozens of different methods have evolved for rigging baits for trolling. As is the case with offshore artificial lures, if and when you make an offshore charter, the skipper and mate on the sport-fishing boat will be rigging the trolling baits. Your direct knowledge of how this is done isn't quite as important as with inshore fisheries where you're on your own. There's a real art to rigging ballyhoo, bonita, or other offshore baits to make them swim naturally when trolled, so don't be afraid to ask questions when you have the opportunity.

STRIPED BASS

These hard-fighting fish also make exceptional eating and will sometimes respond to almost any bait or lure—all of which has combined to make them a popular game fish since well before the Civil War. When in season, they are found along North America's Atlantic Coast from the Canadian Maritime Provinces south to Florida. They were successfully introduced to North America's Pacific Coast, where they're sought along the coast near San Francisco and within San Francisco Bay itself. Stripers, or rockfish as they're sometimes called, are anadromous, which means that they leave salt water in late winter or very early spring to spawn in larger freshwater rivers and estuaries. The major Atlantic populations use the Hudson River and various tributaries of Chesapeake Bay for this purpose, and they migrate out along the coastlines from late spring to late fall.

Stripers, as with many saltwater fish, are subject to wide swings in natural population cycles. The late 1970s saw the lowest stocks in many years, a fact probably aggravated by pollution of the stripers' spawning areas. Strict regulation of both sport and commercial fisheries ensued, and for the past few seasons striped-bass populations have rebounded.

Shallow bays and estuaries are home to smaller bass up to 10 pounds (4.5 kg) or so, where they're often taken with casting, spinning, or fly tackle and small swimming plugs or streamer flies, especially in areas where there's some tidal current. Larger fish usually frequent deeper channels and surf areas, and they are sought with correspondingly heavier tackle such as a 20-pound-test (9-kg-test) surf-spinning outfit, or a 12-weight fly outfit if weather and wind permit. Feeding fish may be evident by their swirls and splashes as they take herring or sand eels, but more fish are caught just by blind-casting in likely areas. Popular lures include the Pencil Popper for surface fishing or a big Atom Swimmer retrieved slowly just under the surface. Various natural baits are used, with live eels being the most consistent producers. Stripers are largely nocturnal, and the best fishing in shallow inshore waters is usually after dark, when the fish have moved in from deeper water to feed. These fish have been recorded to 125 pounds (56.6 kg), but a 50- to 60-pound (22.6- to 27-kg) striper should be regarded as the fish of a lifetime. Catches of 5- to 15-pound (2.3- to 6.8-kg) stripers are common.

When we finally got the gaff into him, he hadn't a kick left. To be perfectly honest about it, I was in much the same condition.

— George Bonbright, on landing a tarpon

Chapter 10
Saltwater Flies

For the past several years, saltwater fly fishing has grown more rapidly than any other form of light-tackle saltwater angling, and with that growth has come an explosion in the number of different flies used for different saltwater game fish. A saltwater fly angler's life used to be fairly simple, even back in the 1940s when pioneering anglers such as Joe Brooks started popularizing fly fishing for bonefish on the tropical flats; at this time a small white bucktail was the only fly widely used for these fish. Now there are flies designed specifically to imitate small crabs and others that look like shrimp. There are sea-worm flies, eel flies, herring flies, sand-eel flies—the list is almost endless. The secret to sorting out the whole business for your own fishing is first deciding where you'll be and what species you'll be after. Then you should be able to whittle down the list to about six patterns or so. This chapter will help you do just that.

Most saltwater flies are tied on stainless-steel hooks such as Mustad's model 34007 in a wide variety of sizes. Regardless of hook type, however, make sure you let your flies dry out before putting them away to minimize corrosion and discoloration caused by salt water. I also suggest that you make all of your saltwater flies barbless by pinching down the barb with pliers. If you accidentally hook yourself while casting in the wind, you'll be able to free yourself more easily. A barbless hook also penetrates the mouth of the fish better on the strike. Be sure, of course, to make your fly hooks needle sharp with a small file or other hook sharpener.

These are tarpon flies.

Because saltwater fly fishing is not really done in England and done on a smaller scale in Australia, we'll take a look at the sport in North American waters.

PACIFIC NORTHWEST

Although there are some specialized fisheries for striped bass, sea-run cutthroat trout, and surf perch in the region, the main target of many fly-rodders who frequent inshore waters is coho salmon, which are available in some areas throughout the year. The written record of coho fly fishing in the Puget Sound area extends back at least to 1876, although the sport didn't really become popular until after the 1940s when Roderick Haig-Brown, the late Canadian writer, helped to popularize it in British Columbia.

At certain times of the year, coho feed heavily on candlefish, herring, and other bait fish, making streamer flies mandatory. Some of the older standard patterns include Discovery Optic bucktails and the Lambuth Candlefish. The latter fly is named after Letcher Lambuth, a northwestern fly-rodder who studied saltwater baitfish in special aquariums he built during the 1930s, and whose fly patterns, as a result, are especially effective.

WEST COAST

Fly anglers in the San Francisco area have an excellent striped-bass fishery both in the bay and up and down the Pacific coast. Striper flies are described in the Northeastern section of this chapter.

Farther south, near Los Angeles and San Diego, some fly anglers have made a specialty of fly rodding for bonita, a small and very powerful member of the tuna family. In general, these fish are partial to small, light-colored streamers and bucktails. A small Glass Minnow is a good example, and sometimes even a simple white bucktail can pay dividends.

NORTHEAST

Some of the world's best, yet relatively unknown, saltwater fly fishing is found in coastal regions from Nova Scotia to Maryland. Striped bass and bluefish are primary targets, and in some areas northern weakfish from 10 to 12 pounds (4.5 to 5.4 kg) have been possible in recent years. Bonita and false albacore may be available in the fall, especially to offshore anglers working from boats around Martha's Vineyard, Massachusetts, or the tide rips off Montauk, New York.

Striped bass are one of my favorite fly-rod

© Paulette Brunner/Tom Stack & Associates/fly tied by Steve Jensen

The amount of material used in making a fly will affect its sinking rate in the water. This fly will sink slowly.

fish. There are times when flies will outfish every other kind of lure. I have more than once fished next to accomplished spincasters whose lures couldn't buy a fish, while I hooked one striper after another on small streamer flies. These fish are especially selective about both fly size and color. Black, white, yellow, and bright lime green are all good colors, but you have to experiment to find the hot color of the hour. Flies should range in size from bucktails about 2 inches (5 cm) long to big Muddler-style streamers about 7 inches (18 cm) long. Fly-rod surface poppers such as the Skipping Bug also work well at times.

Bluefish will destroy most flies quickly with their extremely sharp teeth. One solution is make a simple streamer for bluefish by using epoxy glue over the thread wraps when the fly is made. You can also leave the forward part of the hook shank bare as an added precaution.

SOUTH/SOUTHEAST

Southern Florida heads the list of hot-spots for southern fly anglers; tarpon, bonefish, and permit are the species most often sought with flies in the Florida Keys and elsewhere in the region.

Flies for each of these fish are very specialized. Tarpon often, but not always, feed on mullet or other baitfish, and the Stu Apte Tarpon Fly and the Cockroach are two standard tarpon streamers. Bonefish are typically sought with small flies such as the Crazy Charlie or Bonefish Special in sizes 4, 6, and 8. These and other bonefish flies imitate the small shrimp, crabs, and worms that bonefish seek on the bottom of shallow tidal flats. Permit are notoriously fussy about flies, which makes these fish exceptional trophies. One old standard pattern is Ragland's Puff, and an assortment of crab imitations have been enjoying some recent successes. Crabs are a favorite permit food, and successful imitations *must sink* to the shallow bottom. Imitations that don't sink well are much less successful.

There are plenty of other fly-rod opportunities in these shallow, warm waters. Redfish, southern sea trout, and occasionally tarpon are abundant in the back country of Florida Bay and the Ten Thousand Islands. Jack crevalle, snook, and ladyfish are also common in southern Florida, and all of these fish take flies, especially streamer flies, well. A standard pattern in this area is Lefty's Deceiver in a variety of colors and sizes. There are numerous sport shops in this area, most of which sell flies and fly tackle. Inquire at one or more of these shops, explaining that you want to fly fish and need to know which flies are popular locally.

SAILFISH

Of all the pelagic billfishes, including marlin and swordfish, sailfish are those most commonly available to the greatest number of anglers. Vacationing neophytes in Florida or Mexico who take an occasional winter-fishing charter are most likely to be fishing for sails. Atlantic sailfish, which average 30 to 60 pounds (13.6 to 27 kg), are at times common along the entire Atlantic Coast of Florida and west to Mexico's Yucatán, where the best sail-fishing occurs around the island of Cozumel. Pacific sailfish average almost twice as large as the Atlantic version, and are available along the entire Pacific Coast of Mexico, including Baja California, south to Central America. In both cases, 30-pound (13.6-kg) trolling tackle is normally provided by the skipper of your charter boat, although many experts use 20-pound (9-kg), 12-pound (5.4-kg), or even lighter trolling gear. If light tackle is your object, remember to bring your own and to discuss it with the skipper in advance.

Fly fishing for sailfish became popular in the late 1970s and may be the ultimate offshore sport. In addition to being in an area such as Cozumel, where sails are plentiful, you'll also need a 12- to 14-weight fly rod and a premium reel holding upwards of 250 yards (228 m) of 30-pound-test (13.6-kg-test) backing, as well as a slow-sinking shooting-head fly line to match your rod. The fish is teased up behind the moving boat with a trolled, hookless teaser. When the fish is close enough, the boat must be taken out of gear (according to International Game Fish Association fly-fishing rules), and a large (6- to 8-inch- [15- to 20-cm] long) streamer fly is cast to the excited fish, which in all likelihood will attack the fly immediately.

PART IV
LINES and ACCESSORIES

Just as a professional athlete looks for subtle nuances in technique and equipment to provide a competitive edge, so the saltwater angler can often measure his catch by paying attention to details beforehand. This section covers many of the small points that are often overlooked by most anglers but can make an enormous difference in the success of your own fishing efforts.

As one example, wire leaders are often used for sharp-toothed fish, such as barracuda and bluefish. In most shops, black wire leaders, and those with a silvery finish, are often sold side by side—identical except for color. Most people don't give these a second thought and often buy the light-colored modes—but this is a big mistake. After a bluefish is hooked, for example, other bluefish may swarm around the hooked fish, trying to steal its "prey." The flash of a light-colored wire leader may attract a strike from another fish in this case, which means the line may be cut near its attachment to the leader, and everything will be lost. The simple answer, and one that seems to elude many people, is to always use black or dark-colored wire leaders, snaps, and swivels.

That's just one of many examples of the things anglers take for granted, and that inevitably mean that fewer fish will be caught. Fishing line is perhaps the prime example of a misunderstood necessity, and in the next chapter you'll find out how to choose your line and how to take care of it once the choice is made.

It is quite a shock, even after sailfish and amberjack and sharks, to tangle with a big tuna.

—Philip Wylie

Chapter 11
Choosing Your Line

The technological boom surrounding World War II brought nylon and Dacron™ to the fore as fishing-line material, and today fibers of these materials are standard lines worldwide. Unlike older lines of linen or silk, these synthetic fibers don't rot, and while some care is required, it's generally minimal and doesn't extend beyond periodically spooling your reel with fresh line. Nylon is used mostly as monofilament spinning and casting line and for fly-fishing leaders. Dacron™ is usually braided as a multifilament line and is used on some casting and trolling reels and for fly-line backing.

Nylon monofilament will degrade and lose its strength through long exposure to sunlight. That's why it's important to put fresh monofilament on your reels every season. Monofilament is packaged on spools of various sizes and, as you might expect, the bigger the spool you buy, the lower is the cost per yard of line. If you have only one reel, you'll probably be able to fill it from a 200- to 300-yard (182- to 274-m) spool of line, which are two common sizes. Because I use many different reels, I buy several bulk spools of line every year, each of which may hold several thousand yards of line.

As mentioned earlier, most fishing line is labeled according to its static breaking strength, or pound-test; its diameter; and the amount of line on the line spool. The pound-test rating is the amount of steady pull needed to break the line and is an indication of the line's strength. Since the line's diameter is what actually determines how much you can fit on your reel spool, this is also impor-

Bulk spools of monofilament lines will often fill several reels at lower cost.

tant. Many reel makers label their spools as to line capacity, which may be given as either pound-test or diameter, so you need to know both. The portion of the spool label indicating yardage simply tells you if you're buying enough line in the first place. Unfortunately, most makers don't give a manufacturing date for their line, even though nylon can deteriorate over time and under certain conditions of storage. If you can, buy line from a well-stocked rack or shelf, as this is usually an indication that the store's inventory has a relatively high turnover.

Different types of nylon have different properties, such as relative stiffness or limpness, stretch, knot strength, rate of water absorption, etc. Most modern lines are alloys of different types of nylon designed to optimally combine these characteristics for a particular type of fishing. An ultralight spinning enthusiast might look for the limpest and stretchiest line to make casting light lures easier and to absorb shock when fighting a fish. At the other extreme, a marlin angler may look for the line with the least stretch, allowing him or her to set the hooks with more force. Many monofilament lines have fluorescent brighteners added that make the line much more visible in the air. This increased visibility can be a big help when trying to keep track of your line.

Because both nylon and Dacron™ lines are synthetic, they remain in the environment for a long time if improperly discarded and pose

a real threat to wildlife. I have more than once found a dead sea bird snarled in a tangle of old monofilament. Monofilament can be recycled, and at least one major line company is helping its dealers set up in-store recycling bins for this purpose. Whatever you do, don't just throw your old line down on the beach or wherever you happen to be. Roll it up and save it in your pocket or tacklebox until you can dispose of it properly.

Fly lines are very different from other types of line. Modern synthetic fly lines were developed in 1952. Although it's still possible to buy a natural silk fly line, the labor costs in hand-braiding the silk make it extremely costly. Braided Dacron™ is now used for the level core of most fly lines, over which is applied a tough, tapered plastic coating. For floating lines, the coating itself contains thousands of microscopic hollow spheres, which make the line float. Most fly lines are 30 to 35 yards (27.4 to 32 m) long, which is about as far as most fly anglers can cast a conventional fly line. Typical fishing distances are usually much less than this.

Fly-line tapers, which come in three basic shapes, affect the casting and delivery of the fly. Level lines are the least expensive, but while they cast adequately, their lack of a taper at the front tends to land the fly hard on the water, which can scare the fish. Double-tapered lines taper down to a fine point at each end, which adds delicacy to the cast. When one end wears out, you can reverse the line on the reel to get a new front taper. Weight-forward tapers are used by most experienced fly anglers in salt water because they are the most effective for distance casting. Weight-forward tapers feature a front taper down to a fine point and a short rear taper followed by a thinner running line.

Fly lines are now available that float, sink, or both, allowing flies to be fished on the surface or at any depth down to a practical limit of 30 to 40 feet (9 to 12 m). There are sinking-tip lines in which the first 10 to 30 feet (3 to 9 m) sink and the remainder floats.

There are full-sinking lines for maximum fishing depth, and intermediate lines, which are very slow sinking. Finally, there are shooting tapers, which are short (about 30 feet [9 m]) fly lines that are usually backed by ultrafine fly line or monofilament to give maximum casting distance.

The most useful saltwater lines are probably weight-forward intermediates. These are very slow-sinking lines, which means your line will be slightly under the surface when retrieved and not tossed about by the surface chop. For floating flies such as poppers, however, you'll have to use a floating line.

A labeling system on fly-line boxes enables you to choose the proper line. The first letter or letters designates the line's taper: L (level), DT (double-taper), WF (weight-forward), or ST (shooting taper). The next number specifies the line weight according to the AFTMA system (page 77) that allows you to match the line to your rod. The last letter(s) tells you if the line is a floater (F), sinker (S), or very slow-sinking intermediate (I). Thus, a weight-forward, 9-weight, floating line is designated WF9F, for example.

Fly-fishing leaders are used in conjunction with the line to provide a tapered, nearly invisible connection to the fly. Freshwater leaders, as sometimes used in salt water, are typically tapered, single-strand (knotless) monofilament leaders that may range from 7½ to 12 feet (11.4 to 3.6 m) long. The thick end is attached to the front of the fly line with

SOUTHERN SEA TROUT

Also called spotted sea trout or trout within their geographic range, these are by far the most popular saltwater game fish in the southeastern United States, including the Gulf coastal states and on Mexico's Yucatán. They are superficially similar in size and appearance to freshwater trout, but are otherwise unrelated. Sea trout are found from the Chesapeake Bay, where their range overlaps with that of the related northern weakfish, south along both coasts of Florida, and into the Gulf of Mexico. One- to 2-pound (.45- to .9-kg) fish are common in most areas, while 4- to 6-pound (1.8- to 2.7-kg) fish may be frequent in certain hot-spots. Fish over 10 pounds (4.5 kg) are exceptional.

Sea trout favor relatively shallow inshore waters, especially those around oyster bars and grass beds, where they feed on shrimp, small fish, and other bait. Cold snaps can send these fish into deeper channels and holes until weather and water warm once again. Spinning, bait-casting, and fly tackle are all useful at times for sea trout, with 8- to 10-pound-test (3.6- to 4.5-kg-test) line and ¼-ounce (7-g) lures the norm. Fly anglers will want a 9-foot (2.7-m), 9-weight rod with a weight-forward floating line. Popping plugs, small swimmers, needlefish plugs, jigs, and streamer flies can all be effective, as are a variety of natural baits, such as fresh shrimp and small baitfish.

*Monofilament lines usually
come in a variety of colors.*

This fighting chair is designed especially for handling big fish from the back of a boat.

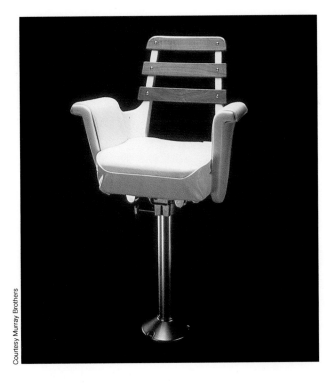

Courtesy Murray Brothers

a Nail Knot (page 123) and should be about two-thirds of the fly line's diameter at its end. The leader tapers to a fine level point, or tippet, where the fly is attached. Tippet sizes are given as "X" designations, which derives from an archaic measuring system used when leaders were made from drawn silkworm gut. The smallest is 8X, which is only about .003 inches (.01 mm) in diameter and about 1-pound-test (.45-kg-test), and is much too fine for any saltwater use. The largest is OX, which usually has a 10- to 12-pound (4.5- to 5.4-kg) breaking strength. The latter is a good size for bonefish and other smaller saltwater fish at weights under 10 pounds (4.5 kg) or so.

Most saltwater fly-fishing leaders are a little more complicated, however. Because saltwater fish are unusually strong, a shock leader is usually used to protect against leader failure from abrasion on rocks or coral, or by the fish itself. Saltwater fly-fishing records are maintained by the International Game Fish Association (IGFA) in Florida, and to qualify for a record, a fly-fishing catch must be made on a leader of a very specific design. First, the shock tippet to which the fly is attached can be no more than 12 inches (30 cm) long. This is commonly heavy (40- to 80-pound-test [18- to 36-kg-test]) monofilament or even light wire in the case of sharp-toothed species, such as bluefish or barracuda. Next to the shock tippet is the class leader, the breaking strength of which determines the category into which a record may fall. This is generally a monofilament section about 3 feet (1 m) long and is usually rated at one of the following break strengths, which correspond to the IGFA record categories: 3, 5, 6, or 7 kilograms. Pound-test ratings are normally given in pounds, and the corresponding ratings in pound-test are: 6-, 10-, 12-, and 15-pound test. This is not an exact metric conversion but does represent the closest commonly available monofilament lines. Finally, a heavier leader butt section is used to connect the class leader and shock tippet to the fly line. The entire assembly, including the shock leader, is usually 6 to 12 feet (1.8 to 3.6 m) long, with 9 feet (8.2 m) being a common average.

There is not a pleasanter summer day's amusement than a merry cruise after the Blue-Fish [sic]; *no pleasanter close to it than the clam-bake...*

— William Herbert (1848)

Chapter 12
Accessories

Saltwater tackleboxes are of two basic types. Some boxes feature cantilevered and partitioned trays that open accordion-style when the box's lid is opened. These are handy because the box's entire contents are visible at a glance. The second style features partitioned drawers that can be slid open one at a time. This style takes much less room to open and close, and I prefer it for that reason. In either case, make sure your box is worm-proof. Plastic worms and other plastic baits contain a chemical that literally attacks and dissolves some plastic boxes, which makes an incredible mess. Worm-proof boxes are usually labeled as such, but if in doubt, make sure to ask your dealer before buying a box.

Make sure that your new box will accommodate what you intend to put in it. Surf-casters who use large plugs for striped bass and bluefish will want a box whose divided compartments will hold large plugs – and this certainly isn't true of all boxes. Bottom, bridge, and pier anglers may want a box with numerous small compartments to hold a wide assortment of sinkers, hooks, and other small items common to this kind of fishing. The metal components of your saltwater box – hinges, hasps, and so forth – should be of rust-resistant materials such as stainless steel, brass, or aluminum to avoid corrosion caused by the salt. It's also nice if the lid on your box makes the box waterproof so rain or salt spray can't get to the contents.

I often travel with one or more tackleboxes, and after securing the lid tightly with duct tape, I sometimes check the box as airline

Modern fishing boats are commonly equipped with electronic navigation and fish-finding devices.

© Kenneth Martin/Amstock

luggage. Not all airlines permit this; you should check first. In any case, here's a descriptive, alphabetized list of what's in my own box, other than lures, that may help you to assemble the contents of yours.

Barrel Swivels: Barrel swivels are used for rigging droppers when bottom fishing and when using lures (see page 97).

Black Vinyl Tape: A small roll of black vinyl tape is good for fixing loose reelseats or making emergency repairs to a line guide.

Flashlight: This item always reminds me of two anglers fumbling around in a boat after dark. The conversation invariably includes something like: "I thought you were going to bring it!" The same goes for spare batteries and bulbs.

Gaffs: Some anglers will want these big, sharp hooks for landing fish. They scare me, as I'm always nervous about falling and being impaled on my own gaff point. Jetty anglers often use gaffs with a 4- to 5-foot- (1.2- to 1.5-m) long handle, since they can't climb down the rocks to land a fish. Bridge and pier anglers may use even longer versions for the same reason. Except in such special circumstances, the best gaff is a short-handled release gaff that can be hooked in the fish's mouth to hold the fish firmly while the hook is removed and the fish is released. Large barracuda and tarpon are often handled by

this method. When not in use, make sure your gaff point is somehow safely covered. Many anglers slip a length of heavy surgical tubing over a gaff point, and the tubing can be quickly slipped off when the gaff is needed.

Hook Sharpener: Most hooks aren't as sharp as they should be, and this includes factory-installed hooks on lures. I use a small diamond hone to touch up hook points after catching a few fish or snagging a lure on a rock. For larger saltwater hooks, a small file is easiest to use.

Insect Repellant: Use a formula with a high percentage of the active ingredient DEET. These solutions can damage many synthetics, including fishing line and rod finishes, so be careful. Many people don't associate insect pests with saltwater angling, but in some tropical saltwater fishing areas the mosquitos can be horrendous. No-see-ums (small, biting gnats) and sand fleas can also be nuisances in the north.

Courtesy Plano Molding Co.

Make sure your tacklebox will hold lures of the size you'll be using.

Lead Sinkers: These again should be appropriate in size and style to whatever fishing you happen to be doing. You might want to carry an assortment of both bank (rounded) and pyramid (sharp-edged) sinkers from 1 to 3 ounces (28 to 85 g) in weight for bottom fishing in rocky (bank sinker) and sandy (pyramid sinker) areas.

Line Clippers: These can be simple lever-type, fingernail clippers for trimming knots in everything *except* wire line, which would damage the cutters.

Long-Nosed Pliers: These are essential for removing a lure from the mouth of a deeply hooked fish. Mine also have a wire cutter at the back that I can use for trimming wire leaders; they can also be used for cutting a hook imbedded in me or anything else. Look for stainless-steel (rust-free) models.

Polarized Sunglasses: These will prevent headaches from squinting in the sun and protect your eyes at the same time. Polarized glasses cut the glare from the water surface, enabling you to spot fish much more easily.

Reel Lube/Parts: Most reel makers also supply a lubricant and often a few spare parts, and it pays to carry them with you. The part most likely to fail on any spinning reel is the bail spring. You should order an extra from the maker after you buy your reel.

Snap Swivels: These are clips for easy lure changing attached to a swivel that can turn freely and help prevent line twist when fishing with a wide variety of lures. They come in several sizes and should be matched to your lure size. Ball-bearing swivels work best, but are more expensive than other types.

Spare Hooks: These may be whatever bait-fishing hooks you happen to be using or a supply of plastic-worm hooks in various sizes. I also keep handy some spare treble hooks and stainless-steel split rings to replace damaged or rusted hooks on lures. Inexpensive split-ring pliers, designed for this purpose, are by far the easiest way to open these rings for connecting a new hook to your lure.

*Fighting chairs are vital tools
when catching fish that may
weigh up to 1,000 pounds
(453 kg) or more.*

Courtesy Murray Brothers

Spare Spools/Line: It's quickest and easiest
to change to an extra spool when the line on
your reel becomes badly tangled or you want
to go to a different size line. At the very least,
be sure you've got some extra line.

Sunblock: Fortunately there's been more
publicity lately on the dangers of overexpo-
sure to sunlight. Cancer is a real risk. Anglers
who are on the water all day stand the risk of
severe burns at the very least. Carry and use
a PABA-type sunblock rated at 15 or higher.

Tools: All you really need is a small screw-
driver with interchangeable slotted and
Phillips-type heads, plus a small adjustable
wrench. Many reel makers supply a tool with
their reels.

That's the basic tacklebox list, which will
probably grow depending on the kind of fishing you're doing and your personal prefer-
ences. You might want to include a small
first-aid kit as well. There are some other
things you'll need or want that usually aren't
kept in a tacklebox, such as a camera and
film. Many people are nervous about taking
an expensive camera near water. I keep mine
in a waterproof top-locking plastic bag unless I'm actually using it.

A final note for fly anglers is to be sure
your fly boxes will allow flies to be carried in
them without rusting. Sticking a soggy fly into
sheepskin or foam guarantees the hook point
will rust and break. Fly boxes with open compartments are best, or you should at least
allow the fly to dry before putting it away.

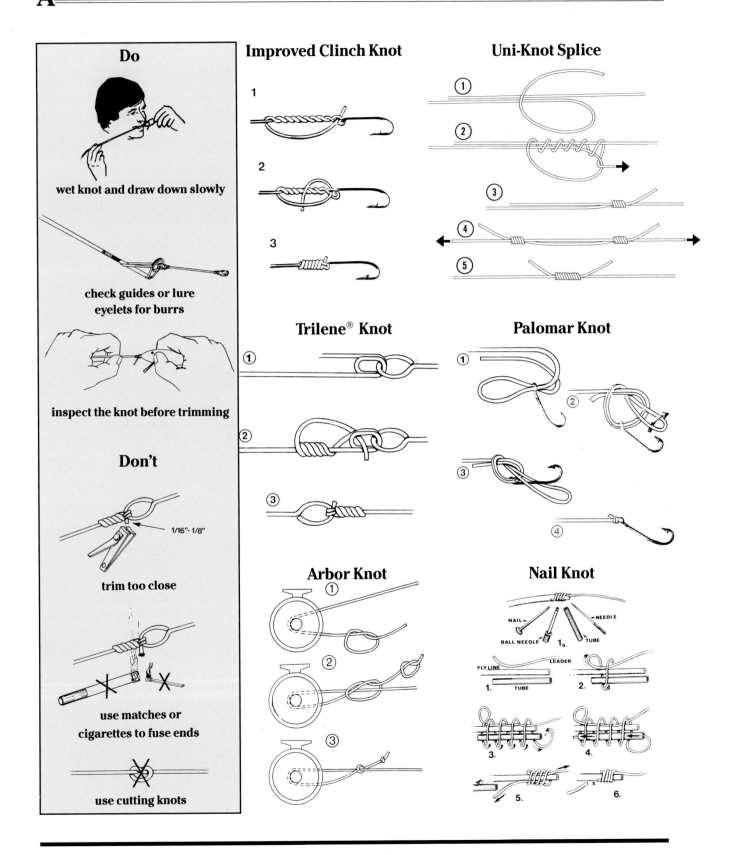

Do

wet knot and draw down slowly

check guides or lure eyelets for burrs

inspect the knot before trimming

Don't

1/16"- 1/8"

trim too close

use matches or cigarettes to fuse ends

use cutting knots

Improved Clinch Knot

Uni-Knot Splice

Trilene® Knot

Palomar Knot

Arbor Knot

Nail Knot

INDEX